The Black Woman's Body Image Diet

HOW TO LOVE YOUR BODY IN YOUR
30S AND BEYOND

The Black Woman's Body Image Diet

MELINDA GORE

Charleston, SC
www.PalmettoPublishing.com

The Black Woman's Body Image Diet

Copyright © 2023 by Melinda Gore

All rights reserved.

No portion of this book may be reproduced, stored in a retrieval system, or transmitted in any form by any means–electronic, mechanical, photocopy, recording, or other–except for brief quotations in printed reviews, without prior permission of the author.

First Edition

Hardcover ISBN: 979-8-8229-0086-8
Paperback ISBN: 979-8-8229-0087-5
eBook ISBN: 979-8-8229-1061-4

For my husband Jeffrey,
You vowed to give me the world.
Thank you for delivering on that vow every single day.
I love you very much.

Table of Contents

Preface ···ix
Introduction   What Does *Body Image* Actually Mean? ·········xxiii

PART I   REFOCUSING YOUR MIND ············· 1

Step 1   Create Your Own Definition of Beauty ············· 3
Step 2   Avoid Unhealthy Messages ····················· 13
Step 3   Don't Compare Apples to Oranges ·············· 27
Step 4   Choose Your Thoughts ························· 43

PART II   REJUVENATING YOUR BODY ··········· 55

Step 5   Engage in Joyful Movement ····················· 57
Step 6   Eating Feel-Good Foods ······················· 81

PART III   RE-INVIGORATING YOUR SPIRIT ······· 113

Step 7   Express Your Spirituality ······················· 115
Step 8   Keep Your Friends Close and Those Who Encourage
         You Closer ································· 131
Step 9   Create a Healthy Haven ······················· 143
Step 10   Pamper Yourself to Enhance Your Health *and*
         Beauty ····································· 159

Conclusion   Spread the Word, Change the World ············ 181
Acknowledgments ··· 191
Endnotes ··· 193
About the Author ··· 207

Preface

Over the years, I've watched more than a few women cry as the scale settled on their weight. I've dried the tears of many more the morning after a Krispy Kreme dozen-donut binge. There have also been days when I've wiped the tears of women overcome with emotion as they've tried to explain why they never leave the house without makeup and still many more who are brought to tears after a makeup application when they see themselves as pretty for the very first time. Sure, this array of tearful encounters with women may sound strange, but you should know my background is an interesting combination of health, fitness, and beauty. I worked in the health and wellness industry for over ten years as a personal trainer and health educator. Then I entered the beauty industry as a makeup artist and esthetician. Thereafter, my career led me to explore the unique barriers to health, wellness and beauty experienced primarily by Black women. These days as a health and wellness coach, lifestyle blogger and diversity, inclusion, and health-equity practitioner, I find myself fully immersed in all three and I'm loving every minute of it. What I've learned is that all these areas—health, wellness and beauty—have concerns of their own, but the longer I am a part of each, the more I am intrigued by just how closely they overlap, and most of all by the magnitude of inequities surrounding them that so many Black women face.

WHERE IT ALL BEGAN

Just out of college, with a degree in Exercise Science, I entered the workforce armed with an enormous amount of information that I was eager to dispense. I was ready to assist my future clients with everything they could possibly need to reach ultimate health and wellness. All the hours in classes, reading, studying, and taking tests were finally complete, and I was ready. I was prepared to make an impact on the lives of many. I thought for sure I was equipped for anything—well, almost anything.

After only a short time in the real world, I became aware of the multitude of concerns that many of my female clients, many of whom were Black women, brought to our sessions. These concerns spanned far beyond diet and exercise, things like low self-esteem, decreased confidence, negative self-talk, and depression. I was surprised and overwhelmed by the challenges facing so many women, and how these challenges hindered their ability to fully care for themselves and impacted many other areas of their lives.

In the beginning, I was caught off guard by these challenges. Here I was the "expert" with an enormous amount of knowledge pertaining to proper methods of exercise and the

THE BLACK WOMAN'S BODY IMAGE DIET

adoption of healthy eating habits. Yet my clients needed more. Many were beginners at fitness, but many others were lifelong exercisers.

I watched for some time as my clients tried to overcome major hurdles with their personal health and fitness. Only much later did I realize that the real issues they were struggling with were associated with a negative body image. Unfortunately, these negative body-image issues were looming over our sessions and taking a toll on me as well as them. I found myself working much harder than they were, and I was exhausted and frustrated. I had a wealth of information to offer, but not the information I needed to address the giant pink elephant in the room: negative body image.

Over the years I continued to work with clients—Black women, White women, Latina women, all women—in a variety of capacities in some of the most amazing fitness centers and wellness facilities the nation has to offer. Without fail I continued to see similar patterns among many of my predominantly middle-aged female clientele: patterns of low self-esteem, decreased confidence, and even depression. Again, and again, I watched them mindfully setting and working toward their goals as best they could. The goals were often the same—lose weight, get toned, or reach a particular clothing size—and I watched as they struggled toward them. Of course, there were those who quit before they ever reached them, and others who missed them by a long shot, but there were plenty more who were diligent, worked really hard, reached their goals, but arrived only to find themselves still dissatisfied with their bodies. Sadly, this dissatisfaction was all too common among my female clients.

And though negative body image is often touted as a "white woman's issue," in my observation, many of my Black female clients were experiencing dissatisfaction with their bodies as well. Eventually, I'd had enough.

My growing desire to help these women, especially Black women, improve their body image paired with my sheer frustration led me on a quest for answers. Although Black women face a multitude of challenges in the U.S.—from the twin barriers of racism and sexism to high rates of poverty and maternal mortality[1]—I realized that without a positive view of themselves, they were ill-equipped to meet those challenges. So I embarked on a journey to gain a better understanding of what seemed to be a crippling issue: negative body image. After a considerable length of time, more study, research and a bit of trial and error, the pieces of the puzzle began to fall into place. This plan for achieving body positive living is the result.

WEIGHT LOSS IS NOT THE ANSWER

Did you know that in 2019, approximately 45 million Americans were dissatisfied with their bodies?[2] Additionally, an equally staggering number of Americans resort to dieting to lose weight each year.[3] And of late, it is not just diets; pressure to exercise is replacing pressure to diet as the socially acceptable means to achieve the slender and toned body ideal.[4] Today, there are just as many programs pushing exercise solely for the purpose of weight loss as there are diets. And though this

THE BLACK WOMAN'S BODY IMAGE DIET

message is not widely discussed, Black women are not spared from diet culture.[5]

The most disturbing part is that while the diet and exercise industries continue to grow through the promotion of weight loss, society as a whole continues to gain weight. Since the late 1980s and early 1990s, the average American has put on 15 additional pounds.[6] In fact, people tend to gain weight after successful dieting.[7] In a six-year study of over 10,000 White and African American adults in the U.S., the dieters even gained more weight than the non-dieters![8]

Yet if you look at the world around you, all signs point to diets and exercise primarily for the sake of weight loss with the promise that losing weight will make you feel good about your body. Think about it. This message is everywhere, and the growing popularity of diet programs, celebrity-driven weight-loss campaigns, reality shows, and infomercials on most major television networks continues to fuel these claims. However, as weight loss sales increase, the multitude of women who suffer from body dissatisfaction seems to remain steady, and Black women are no exception. As so many women continue to diet and fail, this failure to lose weight often prompts *more* negative feelings about their bodies. If as research suggests, African American women have more difficulty losing weight than White American women, then African American women are even more likely to feel negative about their bodies after a bout of failed dieting.[9] Worst of all, these women—both Black and White—are feeling worse about their bodies when weight loss was never the solution to feeling better about their bodies in the first place.

MELINDA GORE

My firsthand encounters with such women over the years, together with statistics like those above, led me to write *The Black Woman's Body Image Diet: How to Love Your Body in Your 30s and Beyond.* However, let me be clear. This book does not promote a sedentary lifestyle, nor does it discount the importance of consuming a healthy diet—especially for Black women, who suffer disproportionately from obesity and other related conditions such as diabetes, anemia, heart disease, breast cancer, stroke, and hypertension. Both good nutrition and regular physical activity are essential for health and decreased disease risk. That's why you are encouraged to participate in both as a part of this program. However, there are far better indicators of overall health than weight loss, and, as I just explained, weight loss in and of itself is unlikely to improve the way you see and feel about your body. There are many more variables involved.

YOU ARE NOT ALONE

So weight loss is not the answer. Perhaps you have already come to this conclusion on your own, or perhaps you have personally experienced something similar. You've read all the diet and exercise books, joined the gym, hired a personal trainer, watched the videos, taken the classes, and even lost a few pounds. Maybe you have tried all the recipes and counted all the calories, and you know exactly how much protein is in a single egg white, and no one can eyeball a proper portion size quite as well as you, but now what? Maybe you too have actually reached a few goals you set for yourself, but the giant pink elephant remains in the room. Why do you still feel like a slug when scrolling through all the seemingly perfect bodies in your Instagram feed or when you watch Beyonce killing it yet again on stage? Or why do you just want to drown your tears in Häagen-Dazs when you see your ultra-perky neighbor jog by? With all that you have done, as hard as you have tried, and with as much as you have accomplished, why does that nagging feeling of dissatisfaction with your body still sneak up on you?

Whatever your goals, until you cultivate a way of life that supports body positive living and become able to realistically see your body, appreciate what you see, and give your body credit for what it can do over how it appears, you will more than likely continue to arrive at your goals—weight loss or otherwise—dissatisfied. My wish for you is that you arrive at a place where you are able to look in the mirror and accept the reflection that you see. That reflection may not be "perfect" (whatever that means) and may never be, but I want you to appreciate all the parts of yourself that are uniquely you. Even beyond that, maybe you will decide that worrying so much about the mirror's reflection is taking up too much of your precious time and decide that you'd rather spend more time doing something that has absolutely nothing to do with what you see in the mirror.

If you are a Black woman in your thirties or older, this program was created for you. It's for women who I have now discovered are a lot like me. Women who are no longer tweens, teens or even college- aged. Women who are grownups with

MELINDA GORE

careers and families. Women who are running businesses and leading organizations, but are still struggling with their body image. We need a plan for dealing with negative body image just as much as younger women do—more, in fact: Because we are *Black* and older, we face more challenges than younger women or even White women our age do.

It is us, especially, those middle-aged women between 35 and 44, who experience the highest rates of body dissatisfaction, and this is perfectly understandable.[10] We are pressured to conform to youthful beauty standards while our bodies are undergoing the natural process of aging.[11]

Added to the impossible standards of never-ending youth is the Eurocentric standard of beauty: white skin, narrow noses, and, ideally, blue eyes and long, straight blond hair. What's a brown-skinned, broad-nosed, bushy-haired sistah supposed to do? Since the days of slavery, society has devalued our bodies and beauty. As a result, many of us have internalized negative messages not just about our weight and age but also about features like our hair and skin.[12]

Thus, this program is not only the result of my efforts to find solutions for my clients, as well as my disdain for the statistics, but it is also a testament of my own journey as a Black woman moving through my thirties and forties and finding peace and appreciation for my body along the way. I hope you too find that *The Black Woman's Body Image Diet* helps you find peace and self-appreciation because it was created with you in mind.

THE BLACK WOMAN'S BODY IMAGE DIET

ABOUT THE PROGRAM

The foundation of this program is simple: Weight loss alone is not the answer to body dissatisfaction, but a lifestyle cultivated to increase body positive living just may be. You may wonder, then, why I chose the word *diet* to describe this program. Didn't I point out earlier that dieting as a strategy doesn't work to promote long-term weight loss or to improve one's body image? And why is it a diet if only one chapter is devoted to the topic of food? Point taken. I was reluctant to include the word *diet* in the title because I did not want this program to be lumped together with all the typical weight-loss programs out there—not to mention the "D" word has gotten a bad rap of late as more and more people have discovered the lies and dangers associated with it.

Allow me to explain. I am not referring to the typical definition, which has taken on a negative meaning. For instance, *The Merriam-Webster Dictionary* defines *diet* as "a regimen of eating and drinking sparingly so as to reduce one's weight."[13] But the word *diet* is not a bad word in the context of this book. Instead, the meaning of the word *diet* in this book is derived from the original meaning of the word, which has its roots in the Greek word *diaita* \dee-ah-ta\, which means the "art of living" or "way of life."[14] This program, my sisters, is a pleasant combination of both: an artful way of living.

The Black Woman's Body Image Diet is a lifestyle manual designed to inspire and motivate you to develop body positive living as an artful way of living, *diaita*. In other words, this program is intended to help you develop habits and make choices

xvii

that foster uplifting, encouraging, motivational, and inspirational living. It promotes seeing your body more appreciatively, more positively, and with greater acceptance. The cultivation of a way of life that fuels you in this manner is truly an art form. Just as an artist creates beauty from her chosen medium, whether it is wood, clay, or paint, you too must find the beauty in the medium that is your life, specifically your environment. I invite you to develop the art of body positive living because your current way of life may be promoting negative rather than positive feelings about the way you see yourself.

To help you achieve a body positive way of life, *The Black Woman's Body Image Diet* features ten steps, with each chapter focusing on a specific step. I encourage you to personally and artfully follow these steps. At the end of each chapter, you will find exercises entitled "Body Image Boosters." This is where the concrete "how to" instructions are located. These exercises give you an opportunity to apply what you're learning to your personal journey, and they are designed to be fun, exploratory, and enjoyable. They include a variety of activities—activities like drawing, sketching, journaling, writing, cutting and pasting, and coloring—to get your thoughts out of your head and down on paper.

However, this program is about far more than following a few steps now only to return to your regular habits later when you get bored or frustrated. Instead, it will provide you with the tools you need to adopt a body positive lifestyle, which includes wonderful things like eating feel-good foods, moving for enjoyment, and ultimately building a better body image. Unlike the typical diet and exercise program, this program has no strict

THE BLACK WOMAN'S BODY IMAGE DIET

food restrictions and strenuous exercise routines that serve only as a means to lose weight. Instead, this program shows you how to appreciate, accept, and celebrate the way you see yourself independent of any scale. It is about creating an environment that supports seeing yourself with appreciation and ridding your environment of the things that support an unhealthy body image.

That said, it is important that you make this program your own. You are fully in control of deciding which areas are more appropriate for your personal journey of body positive living. *You* decide which activities are most suitable to best assist you in achieving body positive living. Your ability to pick and choose increases the likelihood that you will lead a life that you've fully owned and that makes you feel empowered.

This program is for you if you are a Black woman in your thirties and beyond who is dissatisfied with the reflection in the mirror. It is also for you if you are just tired of caring and worrying so much about how your body looks or doesn't look, should or shouldn't look. Instead of being overwhelmed and dissatisfied by the natural processes of aging or the negative messages about your Blackness, you can discover a new way of seeing yourself. Pounds will come and go, but a healthy body image when fostered by a body positive environment can last a lifetime.

MELINDA GORE

IMPORTANT DISCLAIMER

This book is not intended to diagnose or treat any condition that should be managed by a mental health professional. Many women deal with very serious eating disorders or disordered eating patterns. Others suffer from deep psychological issues that affect the way they see themselves. Many of these serious conditions have names like *anorexia, bulimia, social physique anxiety, body dysmorphia*, and *depression*. If you are experiencing issues with food, depression, or body image that are crippling to the point where you are unable to function, please seek professional help right away. Speak to a counselor or therapist you trust so that you can work through these things. Negative body image to any degree is a serious matter for a person to contend with. While this book's message is one of hope, empowerment, and overcoming obstacles, some matters require professional help greater than what is provided here. Please get the help you need.

Introduction

WHAT DOES *BODY IMAGE* ACTUALLY MEAN?

In Atlanta, sweltering, humid summer days are typical, so when a sweat-drenched runner hobbles into my office, it's not usually cause for alarm. But this day was different. A member of the gym shows up in my office. Here she is, a physically fit young woman, about in her mid-thirties, visibly distressed and speaking to me through gasps of air with tears running down her flushed red face, her sweaty blonde tendrils sticking to her neck. Suddenly, I am concerned. As she's trying to get her words out, I catch a glimpse of her blood-soaked socks. My concern grows. Finally, she turns around and shows me the nearly raw flesh on her feet. It appears she has two horrible blisters, one on each ankle, that ruptured during her mid-day run, bringing it to an excruciatingly painful halt. With almost a sigh of relief on my part, I think to myself, "No worries. This I can fix."

I reassure her that everything will be okay. We'll get her all cleaned up. A little first aid and a week or so of rest to allow those blisters to heal, and she'll be as good as new. Unfortunately, I can tell from the look on her face and the reemergence of her tears that my plan doesn't sound so great to her. She begins to speak again but this time with greater frustration and agitation in her voice than before. "There is no time for rest!" she cries. "Please, just give me something for my blisters that will stick so I can finish my run. I just have to finish my run!"

After many more gasps and many more tears, she finally explains. In that moment, I learned that the overwhelming need to finish her run was driven by body dissatisfaction. According to her, a daily run was the only way to keep the pounds off. For this young woman, running was the only guarantee she had that she would ever reach her goal of thinner legs and a visible gap between her thighs. "I hate my legs, and this," she screams, tugging at the skin around her stomach. I can still hear the pain in her voice. "Please, please just help me finish my run. I can't miss my workout!" Sadly, I did as she asked that day because I truthfully didn't have any other answers. There I was thinking that her tears and urgency were because of the visible bruises. Instead, to my amazement, she, like many women I would encounter over the years, was dealing with bruises that were far less visible than the ones I could actually see.

Although as a Black woman you're probably not striving for thin thighs or a visible thigh gap, chances are you can relate to this young woman's desperation. Much like her, you may be all too familiar with the torment and abuse a woman can put herself through if she eats a second helping at dinner, indulges in a heavy dessert, or takes a few days off from the gym because she wants so badly to change her body. It may seem to you as well that no matter what you do, or how long you sweat or how many times you start a new diet or exercise plan to get in shape, you're never quite satisfied with your body. Finally, reaching "good enough" seems nearly impossible. These are examples of the many ways negative body image rears its ugly head.

BODY IMAGE DEFINED

So, let's talk about it. What exactly is body image anyway? The most concise definition of *body image* describes how you see yourself and how you feel about your physical appearance.[15] Body image has as much to do with the reflection you see in the mirror as it has to do with what you see when you envision yourself. It is the mental picture of yourself that you carry around in your head. In the simplest of terms, it's kind of like a mental selfie. However, body image is a very difficult measure to trust because it is forever changing. Your mental selfie is sensitive to mood swings, your environment, even your life experiences.

BODY DISSATISFACTION

The way you see yourself may be negative or positive. The term researchers often use to describe negative feelings about body image is *body dissatisfaction*. This is the negative subjective evaluation of a person's physical body, such as weight and shape.[16] However, negative body image is not limited to weight and shape. Particularly for Black women, it can include dissatisfaction with specific features like nose, lips, skin, and hair.

The terms *negative body image* and *body dissatisfaction* are often used interchangeably. Basically, both give way to that self-critical little voice that shows up at random times suggesting thoughts to you about your body. It can say, for instance, "The color of this dress makes my skin look too dark!" or "Don't wave because your flabby upper arms will jiggle" or "Ain't nothin' I can do with this nappy head" or "I could never wear a midriff top with my fat gut." Sound familiar?

Women with a negative body image often do not see themselves accurately when they look in the mirror or envision themselves mentally. Many see certain physical features as larger or smaller than they actually are. Generally, they are dissatisfied with their physical appearance most, if not all, of the time. This dissatisfaction can have a devastating impact on their lives. As evidenced in several studies, there is an association between body dissatisfaction and general feelings of low self-esteem; women who dislike their appearance tend not to like themselves in general.[17] Specifically, women battling negative body image often feel shame and anxiety about their appearance and frequently compare themselves to others. In other words, negative body image can decrease a person's self-worth. No wonder research shows that body dissatisfaction is associated with eating disorders, depression, overexercise, underexercise, decreased sexual enjoyment, decreased quality of life, and general disengagement in life.[18] It can even lead to drug and alcohol abuse or suicide.[19] For women with a negative body image, just watching themselves

THE BLACK WOMAN'S BODY IMAGE DIET

in the "self-view" during a Zoom videoconference can increase their stress and anxiety.[20]

At this point, you probably have numerous questions regarding negative body image: Why is body dissatisfaction so pervasive in our society? When does it begin, and how long does it last? How does it develop? Why do so many *women* deal with negative body image and its crippling effects? Why do some women struggle with it more than others?

Several theories seek to explain the development of negative body image, but the bottom line is this: People's body dissatisfaction typically starts when they're young and remains with them for a very long time. Self-objectification, body monitoring, shame, eating disorders, and appearance anxiety have been found in girls as young as 12.[21] Even children as young as 8 years of age report body dissatisfaction.[22] The most recent research shows that some children may begin to worry about body weight and physical appearance as early as 3–5 years old.[23]

Body dissatisfaction seems to be relatively stable over a person's lifespan.[24] In fact, it can continue in women well beyond their seventies.[25] So even though you may have moved beyond the body image issues that so notoriously accompany the pubescent and adolescent years, when a child's body is transforming into an adult's, this issue still may require your effort to overcome at a later stage of life.

How does body dissatisfaction develop? Body dissatisfaction is often rooted in unrealistic ideas of what your body should look like, as well as bogus ideas of what your environment (including society and the media) says it ought to look like. We will explore these issues in detail in the first part of this book, "Refocusing Your Mind."

xxvii

MELINDA GORE

BODY SATISFACTION

Now let's consider what having a positive body image is all about. A great deal of research shows that women with a positive body image tend to have a more realistic, accurate perception of their body, especially the size and shape. Often referred to as *body satisfaction*, having a positive body image basically means having a current body that is the same as your ideal body. Unfortunately, only 11 percent of adult American women 45 to 74 years of age report body satisfaction.[26] Women who experience body satisfaction are more likely to feel comfortable with their bodies and, as a result, experience greater feelings of happiness and wellness. Body-satisfied women report better overall functioning, including less dieting, fewer unhealthy weight control behaviors, and fewer weight and shape concerns.[27] Researchers suggest that women with a positive body image praise their bodies for what they are able to do, for what they represent, and for their unique features. They focus on assets instead of flaws. This helps women feel more comfortable in their bodies, even if they do not conform to sociocultural ideals.[28] However, even if women have a positive body image, they still may experience times when they don't feel good about their body. It simply means that they are comfortable in their skin and feel good about the way they look *most* of the time.

You see, according to some studies, positive body image is not some sort of passive contentment experienced by the women who have it; they have to work at it![29] I like to think of positive body image as a beautiful garden. Like a garden, it requires constant tending. Like a garden, it grows and blooms

THE BLACK WOMAN'S BODY IMAGE DIET

in the right conditions, but keeping the weeds out is a necessity. Creating an environment that fosters body positivity is like tending a beautiful garden. Like weeds, you must keep out the things that try to rob you of body positivity.

GENDER, AGE, RACIAL, AND ETHNIC DIFFERENCES IN BODY IMAGE

So, are Black women more likely to develop a negative body image?

Body image depends upon a number of variables, including gender, age, race, and ethnicity. For instance, as you may have guessed, women generally have higher levels of body dissatisfaction than men.[30] Across age groups, men appear to be more satisfied with their bodies than women.[31] It is widely recognized that women experience more pressure to conform to society's accepted norms of beauty, even though men deal with body pressure too. Many women have simply accepted negative relationships with their bodies, as well as the impact it has had on their lives, as the norm. As a matter of fact, *normative discontent* is a term that researchers came up with many years ago to describe the overwhelming dissatisfaction women have with their bodies.[32] In the book *Beauty Sick*, author Renee Engeln describes it best. She connects the general dissatisfaction women have with their bodies to the popular phrase "boys will be boys."[33] You know how men are often excused from behaving badly with a simple "boys will be boys" remark? Society

xxix

MELINDA GORE

views women the same way when they automatically express dislike for their bodies, implying that such discontentment is normal simply because they are women. Horrible, right? It's time for a change. Discontentment with our appearance must never be the norm.

As for age, I created this program to enhance wellness in *maturing* women because, historically, there have been very few resources that address the concerns of body image specific to us—women in their thirties and beyond. I do, however, find it refreshing to see that more and more research is being conducted to explore body image in adult women. Research has found relationships between weight concern, lower self-esteem, and less happiness to be significant for women ages 30 to 49.[34] In addition, it appears that body image issues remain stable for adult women until around the age of 60 years, when they begin to show increased body satisfaction. That's because they start focusing on health and body functionality over body appearance during later stages of life.[35] However, it is important to note that, despite this shift in focus, women in their sixties and beyond still care how they look. They still have a desire to look and feel feminine and beautiful; they just have greater appreciation for the proper functioning of their bodies.

Research has revealed that, like gender and age, race and ethnicity can influence body image. Body dissatisfaction is experienced by women of all ethnicities, but a strong group identity may protect some racial and ethnic groups from some negative societal messages about their bodies. For instance, some earlier studies suggested that mature African American and Hispanic women were more likely than women of other

THE BLACK WOMAN'S BODY IMAGE DIET

races or ethnicities to report satisfaction with their bodies.[36] In general, the African American and Hispanic women in the studies accepted a body size and shape that were larger and more diverse than those idealized in White American culture. However, more recent research regarding African American women reveals that, though they were part of a group with greater acceptance of a larger body size and shape, the more they were exposed to society's beauty ideal, the more they reported concerns about their bodies.[37] In fact, another recent study by Dove found that African American women reported the greatest dissatisfaction with their bodies compared to White, Hispanic, and Asian women.[38] Yet a recent study by *Essence Magazine* found that African American women reported greater happiness with their natural appearance than White American women did.[39]

These inconsistent findings about African American body satisfaction may reflect the limited way that most researchers have defined and measured body image. Historically, researchers focused on women of European descent and their concerns about body size and shape. Because our culture was allegedly more accepting of larger body sizes and shapes, most researchers assumed that Black women were immune to body dissatisfaction. However, more recently, researchers have found that hair and skin color play a significant role in African American women's concerns about body image.[40] You may not find this finding surprising, given the persistence of "colorism" in the Black community in spite of the "Black Is Beautiful" movement of the 1960s and 1970s. Historically, having internalized White racism, many Blacks as well as Whites

MELINDA GORE

have shunned dark-skinned Black people and privileged those with light skin.[41] Clearly, when investigating our body image concerns, researchers need to expand their definition of *body image*. An expanded and more inclusive definition of body image is needed so that we are not discounted and overlooked for eating disorders, depression, and other problems that stem from body dissatisfaction.

Regardless of race or ethnicity, women with body image concerns find ways to protect themselves through a variety of mechanisms. For example, some avoid wearing particular clothing on days when they feel more body vulnerable.[42] Others may avoid engaging in social activities or leaving their homes at all. For these reasons, it is essential that you tackle negative body image head-on because the way you feel about yourself ultimately affects how you behave, how you interact with others, and to what degree you engage or disengage in life. Together, we will do just that in the pages of this book: tackle it head-on.

WHAT IS YOUR BODY IMAGE?

Now that you have a better understanding of body image, ask yourself these questions: How do you see yourself? How do you feel about what you see in the mirror? What does your mental selfie look like? Does it match what you see in the mirror? If you had the courage to post your mental selfie to social media, would others agree with what you see? I challenge you to take the following assessment to determine how positively you feel about your body—and to be honest about it.

THE BLACK WOMAN'S BODY IMAGE DIET

Body Positivity Assessment

This tool is adapted from a quiz titled Healthy Body Image: 11 Questions to Establish Your Level of Body Positivity from Askthescientists.com.[43]

Directions:

Select one answer for each of the following statements.

1. Which best describes the internal dialogue you have with yourself about your body?

   a. These jeans used to be much looser around my hips and thighs. This is unacceptable!
   b. These jeans fit a bit more snugly today. It's not the end of the world. I'll be sure to make healthier food choices going forward.
   c. Girl, you are wearing these jeans! They are hugging my curves in all the right places.

2. What is the first thought that comes to your mind when you see a beautiful celebrity in a magazine or on a movie screen?

   a. If only my body were as fit as her body, I need a head to toe makeover.

xxxiii

b. She looks great! It really pays to take good care of yourself.

c. I love what she is wearing! I could totally rock that too!

3. What is the first thing you see when you look at your body in the mirror?

a. All the lumps, bumps and areas I hate.

b. The parts of my body I'm not in love with, but don't hate either, because I realize I can always work on them.

c. All the wonderful aspects of my body that make me uniquely who I am.

4. What makes a Black woman beautiful?

a. Long hair, light skin and a slender fit body.

b. Confidence in herself and kindness toward others.

c. Comfortable in her own skin no matter her shape, complexion or body size.

5. Why do you engage in exercise?

a. I don't. What's the point? My body will never be any different than it is.

b. It strengthens my mind and my body.

c. It leaves me feeling refreshed and invigorated.

THE BLACK WOMAN'S BODY IMAGE DIET

6. What is your motivation for making healthy food choices?

   a. I want to change my body.
   b. I enjoy giving my body good things, it makes me feel good.
   c. Eating well is a simple way to show respect for my body.

7. What is your typical response when a girlfriend compliments your appearance?

   a. Girl, stop lying! I've put on so much weight.
   b. Really? You think so? Thank you.
   c. Oh, thank you! You look great too!

8. How does your spiritual practice impact the way you feel about your body?

   a. It doesn't. I'm completely to blame for the shape I'm in.
   b. When feeling down on myself, it lifts me up.
   c. It's a constant reminder that I am exactly as I should be.

9. How often do you make regular appointments for self-care?

   a. Self-care? What is that?
   b. Not as often as I would like, but I believe it is important.
   c. I mindfully practice some form of self-care daily, as little as a few minutes of meditation to a full body massage. I get it in.

MELINDA GORE

10. Which series of words best describes how you feel about your body?

    a. Disgusted, disappointed, resentful
    b. Hopeful, pleased, optimistic
    c. Compassion, respectful, positive

11. I appreciate the different and unique characteristics of my body.

    a. Never
    b. Often
    c. Always

Scoring:

Add point totals for As, Bs and Cs together for final score.

A = 1 POINT
B = 2 POINTS
C = 3 POINTS

OUTSTANDING! (29 TO 33)

You are right on! Your present view of your body is positive and exactly what you'll need to support a healthy body image. You're on the right track!

GREAT! (23 TO 28)

Your ability to accept that your body is always changing will serve you well in overcoming any measure of dissatisfaction you have with your body.

GOOD (16 TO 22)

When it comes to seeing your body positively, you are a work in progress. The good news is you are building on a solid foundation. A healthy body image is within reach.

MELINDA GORE

NEEDS IMPROVEMENT (14 OR LESS)

Nothing beats failure but a try. You have your work cut out for you in order to see your body more positively, but don't be discouraged. This book and other resources like it are a great place to begin the journey.

So, how did you do? Regardless of your score or the answers to the questions from before, please do not take either lightly. What new information have you discovered? Any surprises? Take some time to think about your responses. It is often the thinking that takes place before the doing that really makes the difference. If you do not, wouldn't you like to see yourself in a more positive light, to appreciate all of the wonderful qualities that make you the person you are? Please understand, no woman is fully satisfied with her body one hundred percent of the time. What is most important is that, by following the steps in this book, you can develop a healthier, more realistic appreciation for your body, and you can become more satisfied with your appearance and more engaged in your life as a result. The bonus of making new connections with people and uncovering new activities that bring you enjoyment is just the frosting on an already delicious cake.

BODY IMAGE BOOSTER: CREATE THE VISION

I encourage you to begin this journey toward greater body positivity with the end in mind. Envision your life at some point in the future. If your negative thoughts about your body are magically erased, what do you look like? What is your life like? What are you doing? Who are you spending time with? What is your mood? How do you feel?

Record the vision you have for your future self in a journal. Start by obtaining a scrapbook, a sketch pad, a notebook, or loose-leaf binder. Find a creative way to label it and designate it as your "Body Positive Living" journal. Get one as large or small or as fancy or plain as you prefer. You may use it to record your answers to all the questions and exercises in this book. You may also want to use it to journal about your thoughts and feelings as you read the chapters and work through the steps.

For this exercise, write out your vision as if it were already taking place. Example: *I am happy and engaged in my life. My focus is on spending quality time with family and friends. I nourish myself through positive relationships and helping others. I take pride in caring for my body. My body grows stronger with each exercise session. I eat a healthful diet and engage in movement that I enjoy.* Now bring your vision to life. There are no rules. Do not allow yourself to be limited by lines or words: create or find a few images to support the words you have written. Feel free to clip pictures from magazines, draw, doodle, and cut and paste to your heart's content. Just give it a try.

*Please visit www.freegiftfrommelinda.com
for printable worksheets to guide you through
each chapter's Body Image Booster.*

THE BLACK WOMAN'S BODY IMAGE DIET

THE JOURNEY BEGINS

At times, you may find yourself less than fully engaged in life because you focus more attention than you would like on how your body looks and how it makes you feel. Let us begin the ten steps to address these issues and work to cultivate a lifestyle that promotes body positive living. The journey begins here, and it's never too late to start. You have so much life to live, and you have so much more to offer the world around you. You will be pleasantly surprised when your work, family, and relationships begin to flourish once you cultivate a body positive way of living.

PART I

REFOCUSING YOUR MIND

Step One

CREATE YOUR OWN DEFINITION OF BEAUTY

I remember my first encounter with beauty and when the word gained meaning for me. I was five or six years old. If I was lucky, when my mom had to be away, she would ask our neighbor to watch me and my little brother. Our neighbor was a grand caramel-colored woman who must have stood six feet tall, possibly taller if you add in her neatly pinned beehive hairdo. She wore colorful, flowing caftan gowns with matching slippers. She never lacked a pair of coordinated dangling earrings and layers of beaded necklaces and bangle bracelets. Oh, how I loved the soothing sound of her bangles clicking together as she floated gracefully around our backyard! She dazzled us for hours with songs and tales of romance. I can't decide what mesmerized me most: her expertly applied makeup—complete with false lashes and the brightest shades of lipstick against her strikingly white teeth—or the caftans or her flowery fragrance that I always caught a whiff of in the wind. No doubt about it,

MELINDA GORE

this woman personified beauty, and my six-year-old self always thought that one day, if I could ever grow tall enough, I wanted to look just like her.

You may not realize it, but many of the opinions that we as adult women hold concerning beauty and appearance began in our childhood. Since then, if we were not given a realistic defini-tion of beauty or weren't exposed to more inclusive examples of beauty, we probably adopted society's narrow definition. So the first step in your journey toward body positive living focuses on creating a new definition of beauty.

MOM, WHERE DOES BEAUTY COME FROM?

Ask just about anyone on the streets of America what their idea of beauty is, and more likely than not, they'll give you an answer consistent with that of the "ideal female" featured in the mass media: prototypically young, tall, thin, and White, with at least moderately large breasts.[44] As disturbing as this is, if you flip through any magazine or watch any television program, you will likely see the same.

Do you know where your perceptions of beauty come from? Where your earliest ideas of beauty originated? Was the term *beauty* used freely in your home when you were a child? Did your parents or siblings openly differentiate between "beautiful" and "not beautiful," especially when it came to describing people? Was the word used only to describe appearance-related traits, or was it used to describe non-aesthetic characteristics as well?

THE BLACK WOMAN'S BODY IMAGE DIET

Reflecting on our earliest notions around the abstract concept of beauty gives us quite a lot to consider.

It's interesting. I'll bet if you ask my brother to describe our neighbor, his recollection would be much different from mine. The point is, however it happened, we have each arrived at a definition of beauty. Has your definition changed over the years? With life experiences? With age? How has your concept of beauty evolved? An old saying goes "Beauty is in the eye of the beholder," but I wonder just how true that statement is in today's society. Here in the United States, we are a melting pot of all kinds of people. Just look around you. All sizes, shapes, ages, body types, ethnicities, hair colors, skin colors, and eye colors are represented in abundance everywhere—except in our media. The commercialized version of beauty that we see daily remains virtually the same. Despite all the efforts exerted by women's activists who lobby for change, the beauty narrative mostly remains stagnant, with only slight variations on the same theme.

It's important for me as a Black woman in my forties to see representations in the media of women who look like me. In fact, women and girls of all ages are positively impacted when they see faces like their own in prominent places. I recall a little game my sister and I played when we were younger. My mother would get the JCPenney catalog around the holidays so that we could go through it and make our Christmas lists for Santa. It was a very exciting time in the Gore home when the catalog arrived. My siblings and I would pore over the pages, wishing and waiting excitedly for Christmas Day.

MELINDA GORE

After our lists were made and we felt confident that our requests would be delivered to the Big Guy in time, my sister and I would snuggle side by side in my father's old rocking chair, the heavy catalog resting on our knees. We eagerly flipped through every page of that catalog, counting the number of African American models on each page. If an African American model appeared on the right side, where my sister sat, she earned a point. If one appeared on the left side, the point went to me. At the end of the game, whoever had the most points was the winner. As I think back, the most either of us ever scored was around nine or ten points, and there were surely times when we just gave up because the points were so few and far between. After many years of this game, I realized the point totals weren't increasing by much. At about the same time, I realized we were counting the same model over and over again. It is still an unfortunate reality.

With such limited representations of beauty surrounding us, it's easy to just accept the status quo. But here are some questions for you: Do you agree with society's definition of beauty? Have you ever thought about it? Do you simply accept society's definition because you have never taken the time to define beauty for yourself? If you haven't, why not?

Just for a moment, let's remove the media, our parents, even the JCPenney catalog from the equation. Who decides what is beautiful to *you*? *Merriam-Webster's* definition of *beautiful* is "generally pleasing," but what do you think?[45] When it comes to people, who is to say what is and what is not beautiful? Why is there such a narrow representation of beauty in the media in the first place? Why is the average model in the 2000s thinner

THE BLACK WOMAN'S BODY IMAGE DIET

than 98 percent of U.S. women?[46] I can think of many things that make a woman beautiful, both aesthetically and otherwise. I can also think of many things that have very little to do with size or weight. Consider all these things, because this is how you begin to create your new definition of beauty.

This step is included as a part of the program because I want you to start thinking about your own definition of beauty and deliberately reminding yourself of it often. Take into account where it is currently and how it changes as you embark on your journey of body positive living. Make notes in your Body Positive Living journal along the way; put your thoughts and ideas into words. *This is a very important step toward body positive living, and it is one that should not be omitted.*

But before we begin, I would be remiss not to mention the unevenness of the playing field. Women are held to a much higher standard of beauty than are men. Furthermore, notice how women are described in terms of their appearance while men are described as "strong," "powerful," and "smart." Granted, more men today are going in for little nips and tucks than ever before, but women are still pressured to keep the beauty bar set to unrealistic heights. These unrealistically high standards contribute to many of the issues that women have with their appearance. That's why I am empowering you to decide what beauty means to you.

Take a moment to consider your first meaningful experience with beauty. Where did the message originate? Consider more than just your initial exposure to beauty, but also ponder this: What does the word *beautiful* mean to you today in your thirty-, forty-, fifty-year-old or beyond body? What does it mean to you as a Black woman? Armed with this new information, begin to narrow down your new and improved definition of beauty. Here are just a few things to keep in mind.

CONSIDERATIONS FOR YOUR DEFINITION OF BEAUTY

As you begin to craft your new definition of beauty, consider these guidelines.

> **Be more inclusive.** Appreciating many types of beauty requires expanding the definition of beauty and making it more inclusive. Every culture has something to offer. I applaud attempts like Dove's "Real Beauty" campaign[47], L'Oreal Paris and British Vogue's special edition celebrating women over 50[48], the *Dark Girls* Documentary on OWN and Lizzo's body positivity platform[49] to expand our society's definition of beauty. Inclusion is important. Seek opportunities to live a more inclusive definition of beauty. Look for beauty in someone whose body contrasts with society's limited definition of beauty—and then compliment her. We need to see more diverse images of women to loudly remind us that "beautiful" exists in many different packages.

Express yourself. How lucky are we? As women, we can easily change our looks with clothing and makeup and accessories and so many other things. Beauty should be about self-expression, whether you express your individuality by sporting three-inch nails, an African head wrap, or a diamond nose ring. Do whatever makes you *you*. And feel great while doing so. To express who you are is liberating. The more accepting we are of our own ability to express ourselves, the more accepting we become of others. Living in a cookie-cutter world where everyone looks the same would be terribly boring. Take every opportunity to express yourself. A truly accurate definition of beauty must include self-expression.

Consider non-aesthetic characteristics. Personalizing your definition of beauty to include characteristics that have nothing to do with appearance will make it more real to you. This does not mean that you must exclude physical characteristics altogether. However, it is important to include a healthy amount of non-aesthetic qualities in your definition of beauty. Consider this: Have you ever heard anyone eulogize a loved one with comments about how thin or fit she was or how she was always a size four? I don't think so. Consider the qualities that stand the test of time; they are truly what's most important. If you are at a loss for ideas, consider words like *honesty, integrity, sense of humor, loving, caring, appreciative, helpful*. There are many more. Imagine the qualities you would like people to notice and appreciate about you or your children.

MELINDA GORE

Change the focus. Focus on what a woman achieves, not how she looks. Consider this as an important component of your new definition of beauty. I have found that often the greatest achievements are accompanied by many of those non-aesthetic characteristics we just spoke about, like *honesty* and *integrity*. There is beauty in starting a nonprofit, running a marathon, raising healthy and happy children, volunteering, and serving others.

Now that you have the bones of your new definition of beauty, I want you to protect it from the onslaught of unhealthy messages about beauty that you encounter every day. In the next chapter, we'll explore how to do that.

BODY IMAGE BOOSTER: A BEAUTIFUL LIST

In order to expand your definition of beauty, imagine a woman you admire. This may be a celebrity, a co-worker, a neighbor, a family member, or a friend. Perhaps you know her personally, but that is not a requirement. In your Body Positive Living journal, begin making a list of all the qualities that describe her: how she carries herself, the way she interacts with others, and things others say about her. Highlight all the things you admire most about her, but do not use any aesthetic descriptors. Once you have a nice long list, put it someplace where you can see it often. Place it close to your mirror. Each time you look at yourself, begin to see those qualities in yourself. If you find that you do not see those qualities in yourself, begin to cultivate a few that you *would* like to see. This is the beginning of your new definition of beauty.

Step Two

AVOID UNHEALTHY MESSAGES

No doubt about it, our society has become one of selfies and social media posts. C'mon, you know the drill. You're all dressed up to meet friends for a night out, but first, a selfie. Why not? You're wearing the perfect outfit that flatters your neckline and highlights your face beautifully. The lighting is good. Just the right pose, a wonderfully coordinated background, just a few test shots, et voila! The perfect selfie. Don't forget the filter. Gorgeous! Sound familiar? Taking selfies has practically become America's new favorite pastime. And this pastime is not limited to tweens and teens either. With all this selfie madness, women appear more confident than ever before, proudly putting their best foot forward for the whole world to see with just a tap of their finger.

For real? Is the constant posting and sharing on social media helping or hurting the way we feel about our bodies? Is it enhancing our body positive living or diminishing it? As women,

MELINDA GORE

our relationships with our bodies are more complex than ever before. The media—which includes social media, magazines, television, movies, the internet, commercials and just about everything else you can possibly think of—is huge business. Images of beautiful, tall, slender women are used to persuade us to purchase any number of products from pantyhose to toothpaste. Jean Kilbourne, pioneering activist, author, and ad critic, has estimated that the average American encounters 3,000 advertisements every day and spends a total of two years watching TV commercials in their lifetime.[50] As you may have noticed, this constant parade of messages suggests that we are in need of improvement, that we should fall in line and conform to socially accepted norms of beauty. Unfortunately, these messages and your exposure to them have a significant impact on your body image.

MESSAGES, MESSAGES, EVERYWHERE

The second step toward body positive living involves becoming aware of the multitude of messages coming from every direction and their impact on the way you see and feel about your body. Look around you. No matter where you turn, the images of gorgeous, thin, youthful, leggy models and celebrities are everywhere. They are on the pages of every magazine you read. They are on billboards on every corner. They're on television commercials, television shows, movies, social media, and streaming across the internet. They're even on the news.

THE BLACK WOMAN'S BODY IMAGE DIET

Seriously, their images appear on buildings and buses and on the covers of magazines at every neighborhood bodega. Now look a bit closer and you will notice that the images all around you communicate a very specific ideal of socially acceptable beauty. Unfortunately, it is a very narrow definition of beauty, and most women do not resemble the images portrayed. Remember fashion models in the 2000s are thinner than 98 percent of US women.[51]

The research is clear. The constant bombardment of these messages triggers a desire to look like the images we see, and we cannot help internalizing them. It is the discrepancy between your body and the ideal body, portrayed in media images, that causes dissatisfaction with your body. As this behavior continues unchecked, it can ignite a domino effect, leading to greater body dissatisfaction, unrealistic goals, unhealthy eating and exercise habits, and negative self-talk. For instance, research suggests that exposure to appearance-focused media that endorses the Eurocentric "thin ideal"—like women's magazines and Western television—increases body dissatisfaction and unhealthy dieting.[52]

But for the more mature woman, it doesn't stop there. These sources are not just touting a thin ideal, but an age ideal as well. The media is obsessed with youth and anti-aging. Thin and youthful images are the norm. With a majority of middle-aged women struggling with body dissatisfaction, it is no surprise that aging can cause many middle-aged women to feel irrelevant, invisible, and less attractive as a result of their changing bodies—bodies that, without much warning, are no longer youthful and consequently no longer conform to society's narrow definition of beauty.[53]

However, for the mature Black woman, the media barrage is even more disturbing since in the media Whiteness is the norm. Although the media has featured many more Black models in the past 50 years, it still seems like our beauty is being defined by someone other than us. Sure, the media no longer features only the Beverly Johnson types of yesteryear, beautiful yes, but basically a very safe imitation of White women—straight hair, thin noses, high cheekbones—only with light brown skin. But often we either see very dark-skinned, thin "exotic" beauties like Iman and Naomi Campbell or slender light-skinned beauties with so-called "good" hair. Just two variations of the youthful, thin White ideal. Are these our only options? Where are the representations of the many of us who fall somewhere in between? Meanwhile, the media portrays large Black women as "mammies" (e.g., Aunt Jemima)[54], the butt of jokes (e.g., Martin Lawrence's Big Momma and Tyler Perry's Madea), or a political symbol of laziness (e.g., the Welfare Queen).[55] Even within the medical community, large Black women are stigmatized as "unhealthy" by the Body Mass Index (BMI), a weight-to-height ratio derived from measurements of European bodies—even though some recent studies show that higher BMIs may be healthy or healthier for Black women.[56]

I am confident that the best way to begin creating a body positive way of living is to screen those messages which constantly tell you that you are in need of improvement and that you must aim to look just like the women you see in movies and

THE BLACK WOMAN'S BODY IMAGE DIET

magazines. While the messages may be plentiful, you have the power to reduce your exposure to them. But beware, for they come in various forms from television and movies to reality TV, magazines, and the Internet. Let's not exclude Facebook, Instagram, Snapchat, TikTok, and many other forms of social media that may automatically feed you unhealthy messages. Believe me, social media contributes to negative body image too. For example, in a study of more than 11,000 men and women, both male and female Facebook users reported significantly lower body satisfaction than non-users.[57] The impact on middle-aged women was particularly strong: The same study revealed that women in their late thirties and forties who were Facebook users reported significantly lower body satisfaction than both older and younger women.

Please know that I understand the allure of the media. I admit that I enjoy reality television, social media, and fashion magazines as much as the next girl, possibly more. However, I have learned that like many other things in my "diet" (that is, my *diaita*, my way of life), to maintain the healthiest and happiest version of myself, I can partake of fashion magazines, reality television, and social media only in moderation. I know myself well enough to recognize those times in my life when it is best that I go without them. The point is, just because this narrow definition of beauty exists, it doesn't mean you have to abandon your own definition of beauty, and you definitely do not have to be crippled by it. So, what's a girl to do?

SCREEN ALL INCOMING MESSAGES

First, you can decide not to accept society's message that says a youthful, thin White body is the epitome of beauty. You can even decide not to allow these ideas in by screening all incoming messages. I don't mean living in a hole without magazines, Internet, or television; I mean safeguarding your environment to keep certain messages out.

Imagine this. You know how it is when you're busy with life, hanging with friends, enjoying yourself and your phone rings with an incoming call from someone who would spoil the mood if you answered. Thank God for caller ID because very easily you can just send that call to voicemail and answer it at another time, or not at all. That, my sisters, is the most basic screening mechanism there is. Imagine if you did the very same thing when those unwanted messages portraying so-called "ideal" bodies try to interrupt an otherwise lovely day. Delete them and say, *Sure, this magazine is filled with images of society's narrow definition of beauty, suggesting that I should mimic what is on the pages, but that is not a message I choose to receive. It may be for some, but not for me. Not today.*

DELETE ALL UNWANTED MESSAGES

Second, delete all the unhealthy messages that have already made their way into your space. I mean this literally and

THE BLACK WOMAN'S BODY IMAGE DIET

figuratively. Literally, if there are publications that you currently subscribe to that bring you down and cause you to feel bad about your body as soon as they arrive in the mail, unsubscribe and delete. Take yourself off the list and throw out the ones that are still hanging around. This includes television shows, blogs, video games, and music as well. Figuratively, delete those unhealthy messages that are on repeat in your head space (but hold on to that thought because we will talk more about this in an upcoming chapter).

Delete those unhealthy, unwanted messages that continue to find a place in your mind—which is a lot like your email's inbox. If you are anything like me, your actual email inbox is full of messages that need to be deleted. When all that extra stuff floods in, it takes up perfectly good space on the computer that could be used for other things. So it goes with the inbox that is your mind. Deleting some of those unhealthy messages allows you to use the space for more important information.

In your email inbox, the problem is that unwanted messages just keep coming unless you delete them and unsubscribe. The same goes for those unwanted messages that come from the media. There are so many false ones about what a woman's body should look like regardless of her age, ethnicity, or race. They flood the inbox of your mind on a regular basis, and so you must treat negative media messages the same way you treat spam. You just have to get rid of them.

In order to accomplish this task, you must first determine which messages you will allow and which messages you will delete. Once you put boundaries in place, with practice and

MELINDA GORE

effort, you can redirect those intolerable messages straight to the junk folder where they belong.

GET IN THE KNOW

Third, it is worthwhile to gain an understanding of how advertising and marketing in the media actually work so that you realize once and for all what you're wasting precious time contending with. As alluring as "the beautiful people" in the ads seem, we (the regular people) must not be deceived. A great deal of work goes into creating the finished product that we see—everything from hair extensions and special effects makeup to lighting and choreographed poses. The final product that we see in magazines is also often the result of dangerously restrictive eating habits driven by the pressure to remain thin. And let's not forget the digital retouching that takes place even after the model has gone home. It is common knowledge that virtually every fashion image is digitally modified.[58] Digital retouching is used to make the women's bodies appear even thinner and their skin look unblemished, wrinkle-free, and, in some cases, lighter. It truly takes a village to pull off these masterful looks. That is what makes them beyond amazing. A simple Google search of "digitally retouched images" will show you exactly what I mean.

Understandably, it becomes quite difficult to determine what is actually real. Susan Bordo, a philosopher known for her writing about the impact of popular culture on our view of the body, observes that the digital modification of images

20

THE BLACK WOMAN'S BODY IMAGE DIET

in magazines can change our view of what a normal woman's body looks like: we see our own bodies as lacking because they do not match an unrealistic, polished, slimmed, and smooth ideal.[59] Simply put, we're being brainwashed.

In an attempt to combat the unrealistic nature of these images, some organizations have aimed to increase media literacy among the people most impacted by negative messages. Because media literacy helps individuals critique and deconstruct the images the media presents to them, it may decrease or even prevent body dissatisfaction.[60] While greater media literacy alone may not extinguish the negative impact of media images on women, it is a vital part of a larger effort. For this reason, it is included in *The Black Woman's Body Image Diet*. When you are armed with a deeper understanding of something, it has less power over you. It simply takes time and effort.

As I mentioned before, I read fashion magazines as much as the next girl. Okay, maybe more. But when I do, I constantly remind myself that the beautiful women on the pages and in the advertisements are not realistic portrayals. I encourage you to do the same. Remember the goal of all advertising and marketing is to get you to desire what they are selling and to desire it enough that you will buy it. It is all a part of the plan to dangle this beautiful, smooth-skinned person in front of you to evoke a response, to make you purchase what they are selling. Sure, your ability to resist may not happen overnight, but it is worth the effort to understand how it all works. Putting these images into perspective may prove helpful to you in your cultivation of body positive living.

MELINDA GORE

A HEALTHY REPLACEMENT

Lastly, it is important to find a healthy replacement for the images that impact you most negatively. Sure, it is essential to unsubscribe from publications that make you feel bad about your body and equally important to gain an understanding of the inner workings behind media images. But finding a replacement for these publications may be an important part of the solution as well. It will help you reduce your exposure and stay on track.

Finding a healthy replacement for traditional fashion magazines, blogs, and television programs is a great place to start. Consider this: One study found that when average-sized models replaced thin models in clothing and fragrance advertisements, female consumers reported a more positive body image.[61] This is an important finding. Imagine how your body image might improve if your regular consumption of media only served up beautiful and diverse women like curvaceous Queen Latifah, natural-hairstyled Issa Rae, dark-skinned Lupita Nyong'o, or broad-featured Viola Davis on your TV or the movie screen.

There are many great publications that feature realistic portrayals of women. Seeking out such publications may promote a more positive body image. Finding one you enjoy will require a bit of time and effort, but they are out there. *Darling Magazine* and *The Gentlewoman Magazine* are just a few. Not only do they portray women realistically, but they empower and celebrate women as well. As for Black magazines, although you will find many positive images of Black women in *Essence*, consider some of the lesser-known Black magazines as well, publications such as *Crwn*, *Radiant*, and *Hannah*.

I encourage you to take some time to read empowering books too. Try out the ones that feature arts and crafts or other interests. What new hobby would you be interested in learning? You may find that redirecting your attention to something you enjoy doing might replace much of the time you spend worrying about your body and the reflection in the mirror.

When you are searching for books to promote body positivity, you will discover that African American literature is a rich resource. You will find autobiographies of women such as Maya Angelou (*I Know Why the Caged Bird Sings*) who overcame racism, sexism, and body dissatisfaction to become one of the most admired women in the U.S. You will find such triumphs in novels as well, novels such as Alice Walker's *The Color Purple* and more recent publications such as Brit Bennett's *The Vanishing Half*. On the other hand, as a cautionary tale, you might read Tony Morrison's *The Bluest Eye* or Wallace Thurman's *The Blacker the Berry, the Sweeter the Juice* to see how self-destructive body dissatisfaction can be.

MONITOR YOUR REACTIONS

Perhaps this all sounds silly, and you're thinking you could never possibly be impacted by the media images you are exposed to each day in the ways I've described. Well, you may be surprised. I encourage you to monitor your reactions when you're watching certain television programs, reading your favorite fashion magazines or scrolling through social media. It is important to learn to pay attention to your thoughts and feelings. It requires you to tune in. It takes intentional practice to become aware of your internal reactions: frustration, rejection, anxiety, or simply a change in mood. Often, they are so subtle that you miss them. Other times, you become so used to them that they become background noise. Journaling is a great tool for monitoring your reactions. Begin to jot down how the images you see make you feel and then try to reduce your exposure to them.

Again, I'm not telling you to stop reading fashion magazines, watching reality TV, or engaging in social media. I am simply encouraging you to recognize the reactions they trigger in you. Earlier, we discussed the importance of understanding how negative images are generated in the media. With a greater understanding of the process, you are armed with the truth. Then, when the images pop up, you can see them for what they truly are: unrealistic.

BODY IMAGE BOOSTER: I FEEL GOOD ABOUT MY BODY WHEN...

Take some time this week to evaluate the moments when you are feeling your best about your body. Is it first thing in the morning, right after exercise, or following a healthy meal? Perhaps it is when you help a friend or when you engage in your favorite hobby? Is it when you are busy with other tasks and find yourself less focused on your body? Go to your Body Positive Living journal and write about your experience. Use

THE BLACK WOMAN'S BODY IMAGE DIET

the prompt "I Feel Good About My Body When...." Create a sketch or drawing that expresses how you feel. Share exactly what you were doing and how you felt in the moment. Keep your recollection of these experiences handy and add to them as we move along. When you are not feeling so great about your body, pull them out and read them to remind yourself of the specific activities that have moved you toward positive feelings about your body in the past. Recreate them if you can. If you are unable to pinpoint a time when you are feeling your best about your body, begin to explore new activities that you believe you may enjoy. Be mindful of how you are feeling in the moment. Keep at it until you find something that allows you to feel positive about your body.

Step Three

DON'T COMPARE
APPLES TO ORANGES

Rihanna, Selena Gomez, Melissa McCarthy, Tracee Ellis Ross, Serena Williams, Jennifer Lopez, Amy Schumer, Taylor Swift, Jill Scott, Eva Mendes, Beyoncé, Sarah Jessica Parker. This list could easily go on for pages. Each woman is very talented. Each woman is very beautiful. But all of them differ greatly in appearance. It is no secret that beautiful women come in a variety of shapes, shades, and sizes. Unfortunately, it is also no secret that not all shapes, shades, and sizes are considered equal. It just so happens that some shapes, shades, and sizes have earned a place in mainstream culture as normal, right, and even superior.

Obviously, subscribing to such thinking makes you less appreciative of the multitude of beautiful shapes, shades, and sizes that exist. It also causes you to feel less than "normal" if your appearance doesn't conform to the standards deemed acceptable. This in turn creates an intense pressure to conform. As a makeup artist, I saw this scenario play out again and again

MELINDA GORE

during makeup sessions with women with dark complexions. Often, they refused to purchase the darkest shade of foundation when it was the best and most obvious match. Instead, on more than a few occasions, they opted for a lighter shade regardless of the match.

In the last chapter, I spoke about the necessity of screening your messages and refusing to allow the narrow standard of beauty so prevalent in the media to alter your own definition of beauty. Doing so is the second step toward creating an environment for body positive living. The third and equally important step is stopping the comparisons you make between yourself and others that cause you to feel bad about your body.

PUT AWAY THE COMPARISONS

This step will help you stop comparing yourself negatively to unrealistic media images and also to other women. This includes other women on television, at the grocery store, at the pool, or at the gym. It includes your family members, your neighbors, and your friends. It even includes the woman you used to be when you were much younger. Research informs us that engaging in social comparison with peers in particular is associated with body dissatisfaction.[62] When women compare themselves to other women who seem to represent the beauty ideal, many perceive a discrepancy between themselves and the socially prescribed standards of attractiveness, which in turn makes them feel bad about themselves.[63]

THE BLACK WOMAN'S BODY IMAGE DIET

The word *compare* simply means to look at two or more things closely in order to see what is similar or different about them or to decide which one is better.[64] Although the act of comparing is natural, it can hinder body positive living. For example, making comparisons such as "Michelle Obama's arms are so toned, and my arms are so fat" or "Why wasn't I born with long, lean legs like hers?" or "She got *good* hair. I wish mine was long and straight like hers" or "If only I had a butt like Nicki Minaj's!" only serve to highlight differences and cause you to feel negatively about yourself. And it is not just physical comparisons. It is likely that women who compare their eating choices and exercise habits with those of their peers may experience decreased body appreciation as well.

I'm sure you've experienced this kind of comparative thinking, so you understand how quickly comparisons like these can make you feel awful about yourself. Whether the substance of the comparisons you make is true, untrue, measurable, immeasurable, logical or illogical, comparisons can be fruitless and lead you down the path to body dissatisfaction.

As I mentioned earlier, body image issues among women in middle age are on the rise. One study credits the rise to a phenomenon called the "Desperate Housewives Effect." The Desperate Housewives Effect is the notion that women in their thirties, forties, and beyond are feeling pressure to look younger and thinner than what is healthy for their age because of television programs like *Desperate Housewives.*[65] All the actresses in *Desperate Housewives* were in their forties and fifties, and they were youthful, lean, and fit. However, the youthful, lean, and fit physiques of the actresses are not easily achievable as

MELINDA GORE

women get older due to the natural process of aging, including a slower metabolism.

Desperate Housewives aired during the early 2000s, but other shows on television today also feature mature women who look youthful and thin. Apparently, many middle-aged women who watch these types of programs want to look like the images they see on the screen. As a result, some actually think that their partners, friends, colleagues, children, and per-haps even strangers want them to be thinner than they actually are.[66] Today the stakes are even higher because lately there has been a noticeable shift in the "ideal" female body to one that is not only thin but toned and athletic as well.[67] Research by Susan Bordo explains that for some women, slimness symbolizes be-ing in control. In other words, the newly desirable muscled and toned body has become yet another symbol of willpower, en-ergy, and control.[68]

While I find the shift from ultra-thin bodies to fit bodies to be a positive one in general (because of the wonderful health benefits you can gain from exercise), it is important to engage in healthful eating habits and safe exercise practices that are not too strenuous. You need to work out according to the ap-propriate progression for your level of fitness, not the level of fitness of others.

A BAD HABIT

So why do we do it? Why do we compare? I believe that like many other bad habits we engage in, it's just that. A bad habit.

THE BLACK WOMAN'S BODY IMAGE DIET

Something we picked up along the way, and it stuck. Social comparison theory, one theory which serves to explain body image, purports that humans have a natural drive to assess their standing in life, so individuals engage in social comparisons with others to understand how and where they fit into the world.[69] In order to make an accurate comparison, individuals typically compare themselves to peers with whom they are most similar.[70] Generally speaking, though, it seems that women evaluate thin body parts and shapes as "good" and larger body parts and shapes as "bad." Although some Black women may consider a big butt and thick thighs "good," comparisons to the thin ideal have basically become automatic for most American women as a result of lifelong exposure to media messages.[71]

The interesting thing about comparisons is that they may be favorable or unfavorable to the person making them. "Upward" comparisons involve comparing yourself to individuals perceived as "better off." Research tells us that women regularly engage in upward social comparisons related to their appearance, and that these types of comparisons are associated with negative emotions, body dissatisfaction, and other adverse outcomes.[72]

As you can imagine, comparisons give way to negative feelings like rejection, inferiority, and failing to measure up. When I discussed social media in the preceding chapter, the negative effects I mentioned happen when you compare yourself to others. For example, Facebook affords users the opportunity for frequent and wide-ranging social comparison that negatively affects body satisfaction.[73] For middle-aged women in particular, Facebook interaction may provide a greater opportunity

MELINDA GORE

for social comparison with friends, family, and age-appropriate peers.[74] Unfortunately, social comparison to peers is just as likely to have a negative impact on body image as does social comparison to unrealistic media images.[75]

To achieve the art of body positive living, it is important to notice and reject the comparisons that condemn you or make you feel inferior. As *Washington Post* columnist Robin Givhan points out, when it comes to such comparisons, "no one has felt this more than Black women." The gap between our natural appearance and the American beauty ideal is much wider than the gap for White women. Moreover, because Black women have been historically marginalized by society, it is more difficult for us to set the standard for beauty.[76] How can we compare ourselves to the White women society has set on a pedestal when society has tried so hard to keep us down? All these negative comparisons discourage appreciation for your body—feelings that have no place in body positive living. Do not allow yourself to feel lower in place or position because of them. Do not allow them to make you feel as though you fail to measure up, fail to reach a certain standard, and fail to be capable or qualified. Instead, strive to replace your feelings of inferiority with feelings of self-compassion and body appreciation, which go hand in hand.

Self-compassion is so important for body positive living. It involves treating yourself with warmth and kindness and accepting that a natural part of being a human is having flaws and imperfections.[77] Research has shown that the more compassion people have towards themselves, the healthier and more productive they are.[78] In addition to being healthier and more productive, self-compassion is also associated with less consumption of appearance-focused media, less self-objectification, and fewer appearance-related social comparisons that can get us into trouble.[79] Self-compassion is important for women of all ages, but it is especially important for middle-aged women because, as we all know, the aging process never ends! Did you know that psychological and physical changes associated with aging and menopause may parallel the changes associated with puberty and menarche, producing eating and weight-related concerns that are similar in the different age groups?[80] Just as we show compassion for teenagers at this major milestone in their lives, so should we show it for ourselves now.

KEEP THE FOCUS ON YOURSELF

I'm sure you have probably heard the old saying that you can't compare apples to oranges. Well, comparing your body to the bodies of other women in your environment, as well as to the bodies of women you see in magazines and on television and movie screens, is the equivalent of comparing apples to oranges—even if those women are Black like you. We are all different with far too many qualities and characteristics unique to our bodies to be able to make accurate comparisons. Because aging transforms our bodies, we can't even accurately compare our twenty-something self to our middle-aged self. So let's reject the comparisons between apples and oranges when it comes to our completely individual, highly sophisticated, miraculous bodies.

MELINDA GORE

I urge you to embrace and appreciate the unique qualities that make you *you*. Comparing is fruitless and counterproductive, especially when doing so causes you to feel bad about yourself. Body positive living means engaging in behaviors that build you up, not tear you down. Equally, body positive living is not about tearing others down so that you might be built up. Let's keep the focus on your body and your body alone. It is important here to note that not all comparisons are bad. I do not want to exclude positive comparisons because they can be helpful. It is possible to use comparisons as a target to guide self-improvement. You may notice someone who has reached a goal similar to one you have set for yourself. Comparing yourself to this person as motivation to reach your goal is not bad. Just be sure that the goal you have selected is realistic and safe for your current situation. The key is to stay focused on the positive. Be careful not to slide down a slippery slope right back into negative comparisons.

Let's look at a few more pitfalls of making negative comparisons.

COMPARISONS CAN BE DANGEROUS

We are all very much individuals. Aiming for someone else's goals can be life-threatening. My body type may be very different from yours. For instance, I may look and feel fantastic at 110 pounds, while someone else may be near death at the same weight. We get into trouble by comparing ourselves with unrealistic ideals of what we think we "should" be. In the Introduction, I shared the story of a young woman who went to extreme measures with her exercise program to achieve thinner legs and a thigh gap—all at the expense of taking care of her body. Too much exercise without adequate rest is dangerous, and it can also lead to more unhealthy behaviors.

As I mentioned earlier, if you want to achieve a muscled and toned body, it is important to follow a workout progression that is suitable for your fitness level. Progressing too quickly and too strenuously in any fitness routine can have dangerous outcomes. And these dangers expand beyond exercise. Comparisons can lead to the adoption of unhealthy, restrictive eating patterns in pursuit of thinner, leaner bodies; such comparisons may pose dangers as well. It is essential to focus on your body's needs and abilities specifically and not get caught up trying to reach the goals of others.

COMPARISONS CAN PARALYZE YOU

If you allow them to, comparisons can keep you from engaging in activities that you might otherwise find beneficial and or enjoyable. Many women miss out on amazing opportunities because they are constantly evaluating themselves and others. What if, just when you are about to take a leap and try a new activity that might improve your health and quality of life, you fall into comparisons? Weighing up differences can often keep you from taking the leap.

MELINDA GORE

In a study of exercise habits in women, researchers discovered that women quit the gym because of unfavorable (upward) body comparisons with other women at the gym whom they considered more attractive.[81] This is a perfect example of comparison's paralyzing effect. You may be surprised to learn how many women you know feel exactly the same way. I encourage you to overcome the problem together. Get a gym buddy or someone to workout with. It may prove beneficial to have someone at your side when the temptation to compare yourself to others sneaks up on you and tries to keep you from taking a leap.

COMPARISONS CAN DISTRACT YOU

Negative comparisons are distractions that cause you to lose sight of your goal. As with any distraction, they serve to take you off track. Getting caught up in evaluating others and being concerned about what they have, how they look, and what they do takes the focus off your own journey.

Comparing yourself critically to others takes away from who you are. The overabundance of comparisons probably explains why cosmetic surgery is performed at astronomical rates in this country. The twenty-first century has seen a significant increase in the number of women who undergo cosmetic surgery. According to The International Society of Aesthetic Plastic Surgery, over 4.6 million cosmetic procedures were performed in the U.S. in 2020 (despite the pandemic).[82] And according to

The Aesthetic Society, in 2021, facelifts increased 54 percent, breast procedures rose 48 percent, and body procedures such as liposuction, abdominoplasty, and buttock augmentation jumped 63 percent.[83] Although White American women were nearly five times as likely to opt for cosmetic surgery, thousands of African American women were signing up for eyelifts, nose jobs, "boob" jobs, tummy tucks, or liposuction in 2020, and to date there is no sign that they have stopped.[84] Of course, cosmetic surgery is an individual choice. I simply encourage you to find ways to celebrate your individuality and grow to appreciate the body you already have without surgical alterations. In my opinion, altering body parts for the purpose of mimicking the so-called "ideal" definition of beauty is basically co-signing what society says is required to be beautiful. Moreover, some procedures, such as the increasingly popular Brazilian Butt Lift, are dangerous—even fatal.[85]

Now I want to shift gears and offer a few guidelines to keep you focused on more productive things.

CELEBRATE INDIVIDUALITY

Negatively comparing your body to the bodies of others hinders you from appreciating the things that are great about you and the many wonderful things you have to offer. You know what? There is only one me and only one you, and they are both pretty great if you ask me. How awesome is individuality? Make it a point to celebrate what makes you different. Celebrate what your body can do. Celebrate what makes you who you are. In an effort to cultivate body positive living, I encourage you to keep your focus healthy and realistic and keep your focus on you.

GIVE COMPLIMENTS

As I mentioned earlier in the chapter, making comparisons seems to be automatic, driven by habit. You may be able to change that inner dynamic by becoming more aware of the comparisons you make. Body positive living is a process that requires effort to replace old habits with new ones. So instead of comparing, work on replacing those comparisons with compliments.

When you find yourself looking at another woman and noticing physical characteristics that are different from your own, rather than holding those characteristics up against yours for comparison, silently pay her a compliment instead. Give it a try. You're at the gym and you notice a very fit, beautiful woman jogging on a treadmill nearby. Take a moment to appreciate her body without insulting your own. For instance, say to yourself, *That woman has very strong legs. She must take time to care for her body. She looks really great.* And end it there.

See? Not only have you silently complimented her, which is a kind thing to do, but you didn't indulge in a comparison that would cause you to feel bad about yourself. It's a win-win. Of course, like any change in habits, switching from comparing to complimenting won't be easy at first, but it's worth the effort. Aim to keep comparisons to a minimum and instead learn to appreciate, respect, and accept your body as it is.

BE KIND TO YOURSELF AND OTHERS

While you are working to improve your body image, if you find yourself judging others, remember the self-compassion we spoke about earlier. Cultivating kindness and compassion toward others is equally important.

Become aware of the frequency with which you say something unkind about others—either aloud to your friends or internally to yourself—and work to nip those observations in the bud. Seemingly harmless comments can run the gamut from "She really should not be having dessert" to "She is going to have to do a lot more than walk to lose that weight" or "Now you know that heifer has no business going in that donut shop." Statements like these are hurtful not only to the person you are speaking about, but also to yourself and possibly to anyone else who hears you. Those of us who believe the unrealistic and harmful beauty standards of today must be torn down are the very ones who should avoid making such criticisms. When you engage in this behavior, the standards apply not only to other people, but to yourself as well. And it is very likely that when you are critical of another's appearance, you are actually projecting your own self-criticism onto them.

So watch your tongue. The use of words like *fat* and *skinny* may be detrimental to the hearer. Connie Sobczak, creator of *The Body Positive Movement*, says it very well: It is up to every person (of any size) to be sensitive to the power of language regarding weight and to choose defining words that are respectful of self and others.[86] Body positive living requires exactly this: kindness to ourselves and others.

MELINDA GORE

EMBRACE SIZE DIVERSITY

Along the same vein, another important aspect of body positive living is embracing size diversity. If we choose to reject the thin ideal of beauty that is so prevalent in the media, we must accept all body shapes and sizes. Check out the website for the Association for Size Diversity and Health (www. sizediversityandhealth.org). They envision a world that celebrates bodies of all shapes and sizes. They promote the paradigm of Health at Every Size (HAES), which is guided by principles of weight inclusivity, healthful enhancement, respectful care, eating for wellbeing, and life-enhancing movement.[87] A great deal of research supports the effectiveness of their approach. As a result, it is being adopted by a growing number of medical and mental health care professionals.[88] We should all celebrate and encourage each other to embrace a message of size diversity.

By this point you have probably realized that cultivating an environment for ourselves that promotes body positive living requires effort. As we learn to celebrate our individuality and adopt new ways of thinking and being in the world, adjustments are necessary. I encourage you to keep making the adjustments even when they seem hard. It's not easy to go against the thoughts and ideas that are pervasive in our society. Just remember the environment of body positive living that you create for yourself may inspire the next woman to achieve an environment of body positive living of her own, so keep at it.

BODY IMAGE BOOSTER: MY BODY "LIKE IT OR LOVE IT" LIST

Inevitably you are going to encounter comparisons with others along your journey toward body positive living. In preparation for those times, I suggest that you take some time to create a list of things about your body that you like or even love. When the temptation to compare shows up, you will have a list to remind you of the wonderful things about your body that please you. Your list can be as long or as short as you prefer. But here's the catch: list as many statements about your body's abilities as you list about its appearance. Examples of your body's abilities may include: "My strong, ebony legs make it possible for me to hike my favorite trail" or "My long arms wrap around my kids so I can give them BIG hugs" or "My feet don't miss a beat!" Write down whatever comes to mind. Take out your phone and print off those selfies for inspiration. The key is to make *your* body the focus, not the bodies of others. Add to the list as often as you'd like. Keep this list handy; we will use it again in the next chapter.

Step Four

CHOOSE YOUR THOUGHTS

Take a moment to consider the following questions: How many times during the course of a day are you aware of negative thoughts about your body passing through your head? How about the number of thoughts that actually become words that you say out loud? How much of your inner dialogue with yourself is self-critical? You may find it surprising to discover just how often you engage in negative thinking about yourself.

Surely, you would agree that a person's words and ultimately their actions begin with their thoughts. This is why our thoughts and our words should not be taken lightly but rather chosen carefully. Thoughts and words are especially important when it comes to your body image. As I've mentioned, women who harbor negative thoughts about their bodies do not always see certain parts of their bodies accurately and, overall, may not see themselves positively. Consequently, the way you think and speak to yourself about your body can help you to see yourself more positively or more negatively.

One of the ways your thoughts manifest themselves is through self-talk. Self-talk is an internal dialogue that can remain inside your head or occur out loud. It is beneficial when it enhances feelings of self-worth but a liability when it is negative, distracting, or disruptive. Self-talk is like a tape-recorded message that plays over and over in your mind. Whether it lingers as a thought or becomes verbalized as words, it can be detrimental if it is negative.

What are you saying to yourself through your self-talk? I'd like to offer you a few ideas for getting your negative thoughts under control and for starting to think and talk in ways that are aligned with what you want—which is to see your body more positively. Claiming the power that comes by choosing your thoughts is the fourth step toward body positive living.

CHANGE YOUR MIND

First, let's talk about the importance of becoming aware of the thoughts that find a place in your mind and the amount of control you have over them. Because the human brain is capable of processing a ton of information all at one time, many thoughts go through our minds daily, hourly, by the minute, and even second to second. Not all your thoughts are bad, surely, but when you hold a negative perception of your body, many of them can be. Considering the number of thoughts and words that cross your mind and possibly your lips in the course of a day, you almost certainly need to do some patrolling. Saying unkind words about your body and allowing negative thoughts

THE BLACK WOMAN'S BODY IMAGE DIET

to roam freely through your mind are counterproductive when you want to see yourself more positively. With a bit of effort, you can gain control over these thoughts.

I'm not saying that if you follow my suggestions, you'll never again have a bad thought about yourself or your body. Rather, I am going to give you tools that you can use to better *manage* your thoughts and words, allowing you to gradually replace them with others that cause you to feel better about your body. It is vitally important to increase your awareness of your thoughts.

Early on in my career working with clients as a personal trainer, I encountered many women who had very poor opinions of their bodies. I could often detect those who were engaging in negative self-talk. It was almost palpable during our sessions. They displayed a defeated demeanor and often used language that demonstrated to me they were unsure of themselves: "Maybe we should start out slower," "I'm not very strong," "My girlfriend has the perfect body, and she rarely works out," "I'm hungry all the time," or "I'm too tired to work out on weekends." While they exercised, I often encouraged them with accolades about how great they looked, how much body fat they had lost, or how toned their legs would be after some crazy number of lunges. In response, they would often nod and agree. However, many cried during our sessions because they were overwhelmed by the journey ahead.

With the passing of time, I began to question my contribution to my clients' negative self-talk. I began asking myself how I might be impacting the way my middle-aged female clients felt about themselves and their bodies. Was drawing attention

MELINDA GORE

to improvements in body parts (body parts they were already self-conscious about) discouraging them from working harder? Were my "encouraging" words more about aesthetics than about what these women's bodies were actually achieving? Was my ignorance about negative body image limiting my effectiveness as a personal trainer? The answer to these questions, at the time, was a resounding yes.

This revelation did not take place suddenly, but over time there was a noticeable shift in my approach to my clients. Soon I was consciously trying to shift my focus away from celebrating body parts and appearance; instead, I pointed out how hard my clients were working to care for their bodies and how strong they were becoming in the process. I reminded them to give themselves credit for performing 100 percent at each session and for making it to a workout when they could be somewhere else instead. Through my words, I encouraged them to stop the negative self-talk about what their body looked like or would look like with each session and to instead appreciate what their body was doing. I've always had a very strict "no scale" policy with my clients because of the inaccuracies and constant fluctuations in weight, so we found other ways to track progress like strength, endurance, mood, and energy levels.

This shift in focus with my clients was game-changing. Over time, the mood of our sessions improved. I began to notice changes each time my clients showed up. They worked a little harder at each session and with greater confidence. They even spoke about themselves with greater compassion. The negative talk about their size, weight, and body fat became less and less frequent over time.

THE BLACK WOMAN'S BODY IMAGE DIET

CHOOSE YOUR THOUGHTS

I'm not suggesting that simply changing how I communicated with my clients relieved them of *all* negative thoughts. No, that's not the case. Negative thoughts can creep up on you at the most inopportune times, especially if you have rehearsed negative thoughts for a very long time. Such thoughts will be deeply engrained in your mind.

Some negative thoughts were deposited into your mind as a child. When you were a child, were you teased by other kids because you had kinky hair, a wide nose, ashy knees, or dark skin? Teasing in particular can leave emotional scars that produce negative thoughts about your body. In a study about positive and negative comments about bodies, middle-aged women who recalled being teased while growing up were more likely to report body dissatisfaction in adulthood than women who did not recall being teased.[89] On the other hand, maybe your negative thoughts came from parents who said things that were hurtful. Maybe they came from teachers, ex-partners, a current partner, or a spouse. Perhaps they came primarily from the media. Regardless of where your negative thoughts about your body originated, you can begin to create a healthier, more productive thought life by learning to manage your thoughts.

It is important to mention that simply changing the thoughts you have about your body from negative to positive, while important, is not the only process I will be talking about. For many of us, simply replacing negative statements about our bodies with positive ones is not enough. Instead of allowing your mind to constantly make judgments about your body throughout the

MELINDA GORE

day, you may need to focus attention away from your body altogether and put systems in place to redirect those thoughts. We'll chat a bit more about that later.

The rest of this chapter offers four strategies that you may find useful to manage your negative thoughts—both the kind you speak out loud and the kind you simply think to yourself. Believe it or not, elite athletes use many of the strategies that I'm going to share with you to reduce negative self-talk propelled by negative thoughts. You see, once athletes reach the professional level, the physical skill sets between them and their opponents are similar. The key to gaining the advantage over their opponents is developing and improving mental strength. The same goes for you. Nurturing the wrong thoughts and messages can really throw you off your game. But don't get frustrated if these strategies don't come easily at first. Changing habits requires practice. Like my clients, you can gradually improve the way you see your body by choosing your thoughts.

STRATEGY #1: INTERRUPT YOUR THOUGHTS

Close your eyes and start counting silently from one to ten. When you reach the number five, shout out loud, "I am confident!" Give it a try. One, two, three... Did you notice what just happened? Your train of thought for counting was interrupted when you spoke. That's an example of how you can begin to interrupt your thoughts and redirect them. It is virtually impossible to continue a thought once you begin speaking, especially when what you're saying challenges or contrasts with the things you are thinking. The key is to become aware of an unwanted thought and then immediately use a trigger to interrupt yourself and stop the thought by speaking. Your trigger can be anything you like. You can use a physical action, like snapping your fingers or popping a rubber band against your wrist. However, if you are interested in getting your mind off your body, you might say something like, "I'd love to travel the world someday" or a phrase like the one above. You can also simply use a word like "Stop." The next time your mental tape recorder begins to play its negative messages about your body, you now have a way to stop it. Just use your trigger and speak.

STRATEGY #2: POSITIVE SELF-TALK

This strategy goes hand in hand with thought interruption. It involves reducing the frequency of negative self-talk by increasing positive self-talk and incorporating more of it into your conversations with yourself and others. Positive self-talk involves the active selection of thoughts, words and phrases that are uplifting and encouraging to you. It is about actively finding opportunities to think and speak well of yourself. Positive self-talk may never fully replace the negative thoughts that will inevitably come, but it does force you to consider positive things about yourself, which can increase body satisfaction. For example, in one study, patients with eating disorders became more satisfied with their

MELINDA GORE

bodies when trained to selectively pay attention to their attractive body parts.[90]

This finding points us toward a great journaling opportunity. Remember the "My Body 'Like It or Love It' List" you started in the last chapter? Pull it out and this time, select a few items from your list to serve as positive self-talking points. Of course, I could give you a neat and concise list of constructive things to say about yourself, but it would have no relevance to you. You would just be repeating them rather than believing them. You need to really mean what you say. Take as long as you need to select the most effective items. Be mindful to use more than just the aesthetic characteristics on the list. If you'd really like to get your mind off your body altogether, make your positive self-talk totally unrelated to your body or your looks. "I am mature, gifted, and Black" or "I enjoy helping people," or "I am loved" are all good examples. Use these positive self-talk reminders when you feel the urge to compare. You can also use them along with your trigger when interrupting negative thoughts.

STRATEGY #3: REFRAMING

Reframing is the process of creating alternative frames of reference or different ways of looking at the world. The world is what we make it, which means that we can transform weaknesses into strengths or possibilities. It is beneficial to look at your situation from a different perspective. Reframing is not about denying what you are experiencing but rather about changing the way you perceive your experiences. For example, if you experience anxiety or nervousness when arriving at the gym because you are concerned about the way your body appears, reframe your experience in the moment. When your mind says, "I'm nervous about working out at the gym today," actively reframe your self-talk to something like, "I'm doing something good for my body. I'm really excited about working out today at the gym." Acknowledge the physical feelings, which are difficult to ignore and then create an alternative frame of reference that is positive. It is extremely important to become keenly aware of physical sensations within your body. Reframing your thoughts can actually assist you in redirecting your energy. Think "excited" or "exhilarated" rather than "anxious" or "nervous." Start reframing your challenges as opportunities and possibilities.

STRATEGY #4: VISUALIZATION

Visualization is the formation of a mental image so vivid that it almost seems real. It requires imagination to create the most compelling scenarios. Visualization allows for endless possibilities. Choose a place, a feeling, an experience or whatever moves you. For example, I often visualize myself on a secluded beach. I can hear the waves crashing and feel the breeze and warm sun on my face. The beach is my "happy place," and just being there quiets my mind and allows me to relax and enjoy the moment.

Like me, you will find that visualization can be an effective skill for stress relief and relaxation, especially for those times when life is coming at you from all directions. It may also assist you with improved performance and focus. The ability to transport yourself to your "happy place" when you're distressed can help you become better prepared to manage those moments. And you don't have to wait until you're in distress. You can use visualization when your thoughts are too focused on your body, your appearance, what people see, and what they are saying.

The exercise at the end of the chapter will guide you in creating a personalized visualization script that you can switch on to help you relax and move past a stressful situation or replace a counterproductive stream of thoughts running around in your head. The joy of visualization is that you can take yourself to that place any time you need to.

So, what do you think? Are you willing to give a few of these strategies a try? Don't allow the simplicity of interrupting your thoughts, positive self-talk, reframing, or visualization to cause you to discount their potential effectiveness. It is the small things added together that ultimately make the biggest difference. Everything included in *The Black Woman's Body Image Diet* builds on the last. While I have stated that this program is meant to be tailored to your personal journey, be willing to try everything. Don't discount the effectiveness of any step in helping you achieve body positive living.

THE BLACK WOMAN'S BODY IMAGE DIET

BODY IMAGE BOOSTER: VISUALIZATION SCRIPT

Go to a very quiet place and create your very own visualization script. I want you to visualize a place where you are most calm and relaxed. It may be your favorite vacation spot, beach destination, or a tranquil place closer to home that you like to visit on a regular basis. If your picture of relaxation does not involve a beach, select any scenario that works for you, perhaps walking in the park, planting flowers in your garden, gathering around the Thanksgiving table with family, laughing with your homegirls on the stoop, or baking your favorite treat in the comfort of your kitchen. The most important thing is to be specific. The more details you provide, the better. Remember to ignite all five senses. Where are you? What do you see? What do you hear? What do you smell? What do you taste? How do you feel? Once your visualization script is exactly as you want it, write it out on paper or record it on your phone. If you write out your visualization script, place it in your Body Positive Living journal. Make it more vivid by adding images from magazines or other sources that support your mental picture. Allow this script to be the place you go mentally when the chaos of life or overwhelmingly negative feelings about your body find their place in your thoughts.

Please visit www.freegiftfrommelinda.com
for printable worksheets to guide you through
each chapter's Body Image Booster.

PART II

REJUVENATING YOUR BODY

Step Five

ENGAGE IN JOYFUL MOVEMENT

Mind, body, and spirit each contribute to body positive living. We have already spoken about your mind and will soon talk about your spirit, but for now let's talk about your body. Taking care of our bodies and appreciating all they are capable of helps us see them more positively and realistically. As I have explained, *The Black Woman's Body Image Diet* is not at all like the typical diet program you may be familiar with. It is a way of living, *diaita*. It is about creating an environment that cultivates body positive living. So we will not be implementing severe food restrictions and strenuous exercise routines merely for the sake of weight loss. That said, let's get moving!

Yes, it is important for us to be active at all ages, but especially in our thirties, forties, and beyond. And not just for the sake of health. I want you to move because you *enjoy* moving. All the wonderful health benefits of movement will follow, but the research on the impact of exercise on body satisfaction is clear. Body-satisfied women exercise more than their dissatisfied counterparts. Women who are satisfied with their bodies exercise on average five hours per week.[91] So let us move on to the fifth step toward body positive living: engaging in joyful movement and becoming aware of how physical activity impacts the way you see and feel about your body. But, first, let me give you a little background about myself and my body, and where the idea of joyful movement was born.

MY JOYFUL MOVEMENT JOURNEY

I was your typical uncoordinated, slightly goofy, awkward adolescent girl growing up in the prime of the MTV era. Just as music videos were becoming popular, I was right there to experience it all. I entertained myself for hours watching the stories unfold to the music and lyrics of every song. There were many that I liked, but my favorite song and video was Pat Benatar's "Love Is a Battlefield." Without fail, when that song played, I was on my feet in an instant, pushing the furniture back, grabbing my hairbrush microphone, and cranking up the volume. All I needed to hear was the first few beats, and my fingers started snapping. In no time, I was a backup dancer trying to keep up with the choreography. The music would take off, and my body would follow. You should have seen me. While singing the words at the top of my lungs, I danced around the room feeling alive, invigorated, and free. It was the absolute best time! Sure enough, by the end of the song, I had worked up a serious

THE BLACK WOMAN'S BODY IMAGE DIET

sweat, my muscles were warm and limber, and my mood was lifted and joyous. And after warming up with that song, I was ready for more. Song after song, I would dance for hours, with only commercial breaks allowing for thirsty gulps of water.

This is precisely what I mean when I talk about joyful movement. There is no time limit. It is not restricted to certain moves, and it is all about feeling free. Have you ever experienced anything like it? If you haven't, then you should. Everyone should. I challenge you right now to give it a try. Get out of your seat. Here is your chance to get your body moving and have some fun. It's easy! Just turn on the radio or whatever device stores your best music and select your favorite song.

Push the furniture back. Step outside your comfort zone and feel how great it is to just flail your body around in space. Let the music take you away. Start tapping your feet side to side, bend your knees, and now swirl your hips. Raise your arms above your head and really get into it. Feel the music, notice your breath, feel your body warming up and your muscles beginning to relax. You're doing it! And now for the good part, add the vocals as loud as you can.

Now, if you actually did it, wasn't that fun? How do you feel? Happy? Winded? A little sweaty? Great! This is what joyful movement is all about: moving your body in ways that make you feel good and make you feel joy. Moving joyfully is yet another step toward beginning to see yourself in a more positive way, but this one requires that you step outside your comfort zone from time to time and begin to explore new ways of experiencing movement.

MELINDA GORE

The amazing thing about this awesome structure we call a body is that it is made up of over 600 muscles, each designed to do its very own thing in coordination with other muscles and bodily systems.[92] These highly specialized tissues give your body the ability to stretch, bend, and move. Without them we would move more like the Tin Man. Thank goodness, we have muscles that allow us to move—and move is exactly what they're meant to do. Your muscles perform at their best when they are regularly in motion. Your body craves movement. In this case, I urge you to give in to your body's cravings and get moving.

EXERCISE AND BODY IMAGE

I believe that joyful movement is an integral piece of the puzzle for building a body positive lifestyle, and the research backs me up. However, you may be surprised to learn that the way you see yourself impacts how much or how little you move. I have worked with clients who, because of negative images they carried about their bodies, had not moved or been active just for the sake of enjoyment since childhood. I can't keep track of the number of adult women I've encountered over the course of my career who had not been on a bicycle since childhood. Others had never taken a walk for any purpose besides getting themselves from point A to point B. These were wonderful women whose lives were just passing them by—until they discovered joyful movement.

Now let's talk about how taking part in joyful movement can improve the way you see yourself. Several studies report that

THE BLACK WOMAN'S BODY IMAGE DIET

you can begin to feel better about yourself simply by becoming more active. It is also worth noting that changes in how you *perceive* your fitness and physical capabilities may affect your body image more than actual physical changes do.[93] Isn't this great news? Just by moving, you are able to view yourself more positively and combat the negative feelings you may have toward your body.

There are many theories swirling about as to why this is the case. Some attribute these improved feelings to the increased supply of oxygen-rich blood to the brain. Others say they result from a greater focus on what your body can do rather than what it looks like, leading to increased self-efficacy—that is, your belief in your ability to reach goals. Still others suggest that exercise makes you happier and more positive in general; this in turn may help you to see your body more positively.[94] Personally, I believe the multitude of benefits afforded by movement, both physiological and psychological, come together to create a "perfect storm" of wellness. They combine to trigger amazing feelings of elation and revitalization, causing our bodies to function as they were intended. Regardless of how or why being active works to improve a person's body image, I am happy to report that it does.

With that being said, I hope you now understand that regular exercise and joyful movement will help you achieve body positive living. Just remember joyful movement is not something you do if you get around to it two or three times a week. It should be as natural to you as breathing or brushing your teeth. Over time, with continued effort, your positive body image can be the same—as natural as breathing or brushing your teeth. Keep moving. You will begin to see yourself more positively and realistically.

MELINDA GORE

OTHER PSYCHOLOGICAL BENEFITS

In addition to improved body image, every day researchers are discovering other psychological benefits related to physical activity. When your body is regularly in motion, it triggers all types of chemical reactions in the brain. With increased activity, serotonin and endorphins—which are basically safe mood-lifting "happy drugs"—are released in your brain, causing you to feel good.[95] We will revisit them when we talk about "feel-good foods" in the next chapter. In addition to mood-boosting benefits, movement also reduces stress and anxiety. For some, regular exercise works as well as medication to reduce symptoms of depression with long-lasting effects.[96] These benefits are especially significant for Black women because it appears that the stress of living in a racist environment accumulates through the years, widening health disparities with age. To test this "weathering hypothesis," researchers measured the length of telomeres (a biological marker of aging) in women ages 49 to 55. They made an astounding discovery: Biologically, the Black women were 7½ years "older" than the White women, and at least a quarter of the difference could be attributed to stress and poverty.[97]

PHYSIOLOGICAL BENEFITS

Of course, as you would expect, there are many physical benefits of movement as well. As you have already experienced firsthand if you participated in the mini "dance off" I recommended,

THE BLACK WOMAN'S BODY IMAGE DIET

giving in to your body's craving to move feels great as your muscles begin to warm and stretch and your blood starts flowing. Besides working your muscles as they were intended, movement provides many other physiological benefits. Changes in the functioning of your body will begin to take place. In addition to the instantaneous benefits like increased energy, you can also look forward to improving circulation and blood pressure over time, which will cause you to feel more relaxed. Your heart will begin to pump stronger but slower. You will also begin to feel more energized during the day and sleep better at night. Not to mention, if you keep this up, your muscles will become leaner and stronger, and you will notice yourself moving more easily as you become more flexible.[98] Your bones may also become stronger, reducing the risk of osteoporosis.[99]

And while all of these things are highly beneficial to overall health, they are only the beginning. I always encourage my clients to know their most important health-related numbers, and I suggest you do the same. See your doctor to find out what your total cholesterol reading is, including HDL and LDL. Regular exercise raises your high-density lipoprotein (HDL) cholesterol, which is considered "good" cholesterol, and lowers your low-density lipoprotein (LDL), which is "bad" cholesterol. You should also know about your triglycerides, glucose, and risk for diabetes. Check in with your doctor about these readings and ask about your blood pressure and resting heart rate as well. It is good information to have so that you can track your progress and watch as your readings begin to improve. In fact, for Black women, I can't overemphasize the importance of keeping track of these readings since in the U.S. Black women are more likely than White women to suffer from diabetes, hypertension, and other chronic diseases that can be prevented or controlled by exercise.[100]

Just remember, though, information without activation is really just more information. Get moving to experience these great benefits for yourself.

So that you can experience all the benefits of physical activity, especially body positivity, I encourage you to schedule joyful movement activity into your daily routine. Start by setting small, realistic goals for yourself. To help you do this, I've included a "Joyful Movement Checklist" later in the chapter. As you adhere to your program and reach your goals one at a time, the sense of accomplishment that you will gain will make you feel great about yourself and your body.

JOYFUL MOVEMENT VS EXERCISE

At this point, you might be saying, "But I already exercise!" Allow me to make an important distinction between joyful movement and exercise. Joyful movement and exercise are, for the most part, the same things. They both involve moving your body and elevating your heart rate, and you can derive healthful benefits from both. However, the term *joyful movement* describes movement that is enjoyable for you. Let's face it: no matter how plentiful the benefits of any type of movement may be, if you don't get moving, you'll never experience them. As I have learned from my clients and my own experience, the odds of

THE BLACK WOMAN'S BODY IMAGE DIET

someone adopting and sticking to physical activity of any sort increases exponentially when they find the activity enjoyable. When you engage in an activity you enjoy, you're completely absorbed, and time seems to stand still—scientists refer to it as being in a state of "flow." Reaching a state of flow appears to play a major role in optimal well-being.[101] This is why *The Black Woman's Body Image Diet* distinguishes between exercise and joyful movement.

Joyful movement takes many shapes and forms. Truthfully, what is enjoyable for some may be very different for others. People find enjoyment in a number of activities ranging from running to biking to rock climbing and swimming. Others may prefer weight training and soccer to yoga and Pilates. Still others may simply enjoy walking or dancing. The point is, to cultivate a positive body image through exercise, I encourage you to find movement that you find enjoyable and to resist the cookie-cutter, one-size-fits-all programs that are out there. These programs may produce results, but they do not inspire you or bring you joy, which decreases the likelihood that you will stick to them long-term.

If strict and strenuous bouts of exercise have not inspired you to adopt physical activity as a daily part of your life in the past, then now is your time to try something else. There is no better time like the present to experience movement in a different way.

I am encouraging you to move for the sake of enjoyment and to improve your body image and overall health as a benefit, but please notice that there has been no mention of weight loss. I cannot say it enough: joyful movement and *The Black Woman's*

Body Image Diet are not intended to help you lose weight. Of course, weight loss may come naturally as you become more active and make healthier choices, but it is not the goal.

I am passionate about this distinction because weight loss as a motivator to continue exercising or to improve the way you see yourself has failed for so many. Also, it appears that physical activity with the goal of weight loss raises similar issues as dieting for weight loss does. Specifically, exercise physiologist Glenn Gaesser warns that fitness programs with an emphasis on weight loss may lead to what's called "yo-yo fitness," which is similar to yo-yo dieting. Yo-yo fitness is the process of repeatedly starting and stopping exercise programs and losing whatever gains were made each time.[102] So if you are focused on losing weight, I implore you to rethink your motivation to get moving.

MOTIVATION TO MOVE

In the course of an average day, a great deal of motivation is required just to get the necessary daily tasks done. From getting out of bed on time in the morning to flossing your teeth at night, it takes motivation. The same is true when it comes to becoming physically active. But not all motivation is the same. There are different types. There is the kind that stems from outside sources, termed *extrinsic* or external motivation. Then there is the type of motivation that comes from within, referred to as *intrinsic* or internal motivation.

Extrinsic motivation is less effective in promoting long-term adoption of exercise behavior. One example of extrinsic

THE BLACK WOMAN'S BODY IMAGE DIET

motivation is competition, which propels you to measure your success against that of others. Another example is exercising solely for the purpose of altering your appearance in some way. This type of motivation, derived from outside sources, often leads to decreases in psychological well-being.

Intrinsic motivation, provoked by feelings from within, has to do with the way physical activity makes you feel. Words like *revitalized, enjoyment, tranquility,* and *rejuvenation* are associated with intrinsic motivation. When it comes to physical activity adherence, intrinsic motivation is more effective. Simply put, when you allow things from within to motivate you to get active, it is more likely that you will continue to be active longer and adopt it as a lifestyle, as opposed to relying on external motivating factors. This is the type of motivation I would like you to focus on. As you begin to engage in joyful movement, become more mindful in your search for these intrinsic motivators. Begin reframing your thoughts to equate your joyful movement routine with pleasant feelings like rejuvenation and elation rather than feelings like exhaustion and being worn out. Appreciate how strong and powerful your body is becoming with each joyful movement session.

Just imagine: it is the end of a challenging day at work or maybe a hectic afternoon with the kids. It's time to motivate yourself to get to your six o'clock Zumba class. Which do you think is going to get you there faster? The promise that by the end of class you will feel recharged, energized, and elated? Or the stress you feel when you are solely focused on losing those last ten pounds? No contest, right? Let the intrinsic motivation begin.

MELINDA GORE

HAIR TALK

While we're on the subject of motivation, let's talk about hair care because worries about hair have discouraged many of us from engaging in exercise or finding joy in movement. According to the most recent national statistics, African American women have been less likely than other Americans to meet national guidelines for physical activity—guidelines that aim to reduce the risk of most chronic diseases that disproportionately affect African American women.[103] So why don't African American women exercise more? Some studies suggest that many of us avoid exercising because restyling our hair after sweating would require too much time and/or money. Indeed, in one survey of 103 African American women, nearly 40 percent reported that they sometimes avoided exercise because of hair-related concerns, and they were nearly three times less likely than the other women to exercise more than 150 minutes a week.[104] I will not go into it here because I discuss it more in a later chapter, but I just want to acknowledge that many Black women face pressure to wear their hair in straight styles because these styles are often considered more "professional" than natural styles. The effort it takes to keep your hair from reverting back to its natural curls after a sweaty workout is indeed a challenge. It is understandable that these concerns may impact behavior.

So if you are worried about "sweating out" your hairdo or getting your hair wet while exercising, don't throw in the towel! I encourage you to check out websites that will give you useful advice about protecting your hair from sweat, advice such as applying a dry shampoo or a conditioner *before* a workout

THE BLACK WOMAN'S BODY IMAGE DIET

and then braiding your hair, wearing a hair wrap or headband during the workout, and brushing instead of washing your hair after every workout.[105] Please note, many great advancements are being made in this space to help remove barriers to exercise because of hair concerns. Sunday to Sunday is a brand that believes nothing should hold you back from breaking a sweat, especially not your hair. They have a wonderful root refresher, plus many other wonderful products.[106] Also, Nicole Ari Parker has one of the best workout essentials, the Gymwrap headband that has a special moisture wicking technology within the fabric that helps hair stay drier during sweaty workouts.[107] And finally, if you enjoy swimming, also check out swim caps like the "Soul Cap" that are designed for Black hair.[108]

IT'S OKAY TO START SMALL

If you are just getting started with exercise for the first time or if you're just getting back into it after being away from it for a while, it is perfectly okay to start small. You don't have to train for a marathon, hire a personal trainer, join a gym, or even sign up for a fitness class. It's okay to start with a walk around the block. Then work up to a walk around two blocks. Eventually, when you start noticing that you are not out of breath, think about adding more activities. The most important part is getting started with movement you find enjoyable. To repeat an important point, for women especially, when exercise training leaves us feeling happier and more positive in general, studies show that it may lead us to feel more positively about our bodies as well.[109]

MELINDA GORE

JOYFUL MOVEMENT CHECKLIST

Now that I've got you thinking about which types of exercise you enjoy and better ways to motivate yourself to get moving, there are just a few more things I'd be remiss not to mention here. Most importantly, always consult your physician before adopting a new exercise routine. Also, regardless of which activity you choose or what your motivation is to begin, there is a short list of things you must always seek to include when building your physical activity routine. I call it your "Joyful Movement Checklist."

√ **Find your fitness formula.** We have already talked about the drawbacks of comparisons, and that same principle applies here as well. If your gorgeous and perky neighbor is a runner and finds running joyful, that does not mean you have to become a runner to feel better about yourself. Now, if you actually enjoy running, great! By all means, give it a go. If, however, you do not like running, then find something else. Something you enjoy. No more comparisons! Stay in your lane. Your selection of personal fitness choices is a big part of your "healthstyle." Like building a great wardrobe, it takes time. After you explore a variety of fun new activities and thoughtfully document your experience with each, then and only then will you discover your fitness style.

THE BLACK WOMAN'S BODY IMAGE DIET

√ **Try something new—or old.** Get out there and try a new activity. Take a class you have never tried before. Learn salsa or meringue. Register for a hip-hop, African, or line dance class. Try outdoor cycling, a spin class, or Pilates. For instance, I discovered the most amazing class at a wellness retreat many years ago called "NIA Technique." It combines dance, martial arts, and mindfulness all into one workout. It was so much fun. I think I enjoyed it so much because you simply flail your body around through space and work up a sweat doing so. It took me right back to my MTV days, dancing around in my living room for hours to music videos. So I also encourage you to think about what you enjoyed when you were younger. Take up those activities again. You may also discover that you enjoy an activity you did *not* like before if you change the time and place. For example, maybe you disliked running on a treadmill but love running in the park. There are so many options out there. Stretch your boundaries and give something new or old a try.

√ **Make an appointment with yourself.** Schedule time for movement and honor it. To effectively reap the benefits of movement, you must make time for it. Schedule it into your day just as you would any other important appointment you must keep. On this journey toward improving the way you see your body, you will quickly learn that taking care of yourself is a daily decision. Honor the time you set aside for joyful movement.

MELINDA GORE

√ **Wear something cute.** I am not suggesting that you go out and buy the most expensive workout wear available, though it can be very tempting to do so. I am recommending that you spruce up your workout attire just a bit. It is important to invest in good sports bras and sneakers. You have to use them, so you may as well get something you like. You have a little more pep in your step when your clothes fit well and are clean and matching. It helps you feel good about the way you look. Allow the reflection in the mirror to inspire you.

√ **Engage in body awareness.** Body awareness involves being attentive to all aspects of your body as you engage in movement. For movement to be most effective, you must become familiar with your body while you move. Long gone are the days of avoiding mirrors. Watch and feel yourself move. Become aware of your body's placement in space. Truly begin to appreciate the joy that comes from movement. Be free. Become aware of tension in every muscle and the transition to relaxation as you continue. Notice and evaluate what it feels like to stretch and bend.

√ **Rest and hydrate**. As it turns out, getting enough rest is just as important as getting enough exercise. Any time you engage in physical activity, you must be sure to give your body time to recuperate. Resting allows your organs and tissues to repair and get stronger. And don't forget to drink plenty of water. Try to drink frequently before, during, and after your joyful movement sessions.

THE BLACK WOMAN'S BODY IMAGE DIET

√ ***Incorporate movement into your day.*** Take advantage of every opportunity you have to move. Walk or bike to work if you can. Take the stairs instead of the elevator. Set a timer at your desk to remind you to get up and move around regularly. Park farther away from the door when running errands. If you live in a large city, get off the train a few stops before your stop and walk the rest of the way. Squeeze in a few crunches, jumping jacks, or sit-ups during the commercial breaks of your favorite television show.

√ ***Write in your journal.*** Make notes about various activities you engage in and how each one makes you feel. Notice and record how you feel before, during, and after a variety of joyful movement activities. Getting in touch with your feelings around specific activities will give you immediate feedback as to whether or not you would like to incorporate them into your daily routine.

√ ***Create a backup plan for boredom.*** Your likelihood of success and continuing to engage in joyful movement as a way of life will greatly increase if you proactively plan for boredom. You will thank yourself later. Partner with a friend or invite as many of your girlfriends as you want. Change the time or place of your activity. Add variety to your program any time you feel boredom sneaking up on you. Switch it up. The best way to stave off boredom is to keep learning something new.

MELINDA GORE

IDEAS FOR JOYFUL MOVEMENT

The options for joyful movement are plentiful. As you check off items on your "Joyful Movement Checklist," I encourage you to include the basics of a good exercise program. Always start your joyful movement session with a warm-up and stretch and conclude with a cool-down and a stretch. Be mindful of your intensity with a heart rate monitor or a quick pulse check. Also, when adding new activities, always aim to include a combination of strength training, cardiovascular exercise, and flexibility activities. An effective joyful movement session should burn anywhere from 250 to 300 calories. The World Health Organization recommends that adults between 18 and 64 years of age engage in at least 150 minutes of moderate-intensity aerobic physical activity throughout the week to improve cardiorespiratory and muscular fitness and to reduce the risk of non-chronic diseases and depression.[110] This means elevating your heart rate for 30 minutes five days per week. If you are unable to get the full 30 minutes in all at once, you can break it up during the day. A few 15-minute walks are better than none at all.

Here are just a few ideas of various types of joyful movement exercises to get you going.

Circuit training. This fun and effective activity involves alternating strengthening moves with cardiovascular exercise. Circuit training is very effective for the female exerciser. It is also super-efficient for building muscle and burning fat. It

THE BLACK WOMAN'S BODY IMAGE DIET

keeps you moving, so boredom is kept at bay. Studies show that higher intensity exercise elicits more body positivity by providing immediate feedback of an exerciser's functional ability.[111] In other words, the focus on the body's ability over its appearance is key in promoting body satisfaction. One type of circuit training, HIIT (high-intensity interval training), is growing in popularity these days and for good reason. This type of training involves alternating high- and low-intensity exercise intervals with recovery periods of various lengths. It is a great workout because it provides cardiovascular, muscular endurance, and general health improvements all in one session, making it a super-efficient and effective workout. It is also a great way to combat boredom and can be modified almost any way you desire to accommodate your specific fitness level and needs. It's a fun and fast-paced activity, but the key is finding your perfect intensity and getting the most from your workout rather than trying to keep up with others and risking injury.

Strength training. This highly efficient muscle-building activity is enjoyable for many. It can be performed in a variety of ways to keep it exciting and fun. There are a plethora of tools available for effective strength training including free weights, machines, kettle balls, medicine balls and resistance bands, plus so much more. Don't worry. You don't have to buy a gym membership. Instead, you can create a mini studio at home quite easily with just a few free weights, an aerobic step, and a fitness app. For many of the same reasons as high-intensity exercise, strength training is also associated with improvements in body image.

MELINDA GORE

Cardiovascular exercise. One of the best ways to improve heart health is through cardiovascular exercise. There are a multitude of options for joyful movement activities that fall under the umbrella of cardiovascular exercise. Any activity that elevates your heart rate for extended periods of time counts. Fun activities like walking, running, and dancing require very little equipment other than a good pair of sneakers.

Low-impact exercise. You do not need to engage in high-intensity exercise to experience many of the benefits of movement. For those who may require low-impact workouts for health reasons (knee problems, arthritis, etc.) or those who simply enjoy variety, there are plenty of joyful movement options as well. Yoga, tai chi, low-impact aerobics, and walking are just a few examples.

Sex. As you begin to explore fun and exciting new ways to engage in joyful movement, I would be remiss not to include one form of joyful movement that has a plethora of health benefits of its own: sex. A spirited bout of sexual intercourse is good for your mind and body. Done right, it has the potential to burn up to 300 calories. That's the equivalent of a brisk walk—not to mention the beautiful connection and intimacy you get the opportunity to share with your partner.[112]

While this is a form of joyful movement in which I highly encourage you to partake, I recognize that sex has been taken off the menu for many women because of body dissatisfaction, including discomfort, embarrassment, or just shame about their

THE BLACK WOMAN'S BODY IMAGE DIET

appearance in general. There are many factors at play here, and it may require some exploration to determine what your specific triggers may be. Some women have lost confidence in their bodies and no longer feel attractive. Others express concern about feeling unattractive to their partner. Many more experience challenges with sex in response to the numerous bodily changes that come along with getting older, including, but not limited to, menopause and its buffet of challenges, things like weight gain, hot flashes, vaginal dryness, urinary leakage, low libido, and the list goes on and on. Plus, many of these issues seemingly pop up over night without much warning. Understandably so, sex begins to feel more like a task than a treat.

I want you to understand the reason I'm bringing sex into the conversation is to let you know that you are not alone in this matter. Your body image plays a direct role in your ability to experience sex in a joyous and uninhibited manner. Engaging in this way is what allows for arousal and orgasm.[113] So figuring this out is extremely important. Just as I have encouraged you to take care of yourself in other areas of the program, attention is required here as well. So, what's a girl to do?

If you are comfortable, it may prove beneficial to open up to your partner and share how you are feeling. If not, another great place to start is by connecting with a healthcare provider, one who creates a safe space for you to discuss the challenges you are experiencing in this area. And remember our conversation about comparisons. Please do not compare your sex life to the sex lives of others. It can seem like every other woman on the planet is having copious amounts of hot, passionate sex, but that is not your concern. Your concern is finding wonderful new ways to enhance your sexual health and wellness. There are a multitude of resources available that may be just what you need to allow you to enjoy sex for many years to come.

More ideas. Truly, the options for joyful movement are endless. There are Pilates, Zumba, Jazzercise, stretching, walking, running, rollerblading, surfing, paddle boarding, roller skating, salsa, meringue, African Dance, step aerobics, spin, swing dance, ballroom dance, swimming, softball, kickball, baseball, flag football, NIA, walking the dog, and gardening. The important thing is to find movement you enjoy.

BODY IMAGE BOOSTER: FINDING YOUR MOTIVATION

As you begin experimenting with new forms of physical activity, I want you to do a little brainstorming. Make a list of your intrinsic motivators to exercise. What is it that inspires you to continue showing up to your joyful movement sessions? Pay very close attention to the types of activity that you are naturally drawn to and enjoy the most. Do you enjoy exercising outside surrounded by nature? Do you prefer an indoor studio or gym? Are you energized by working out alone, or do you prefer working out alongside friends? Write down everything that comes to mind. The only rule is there are no rules. You may find that as you engage in new activities, you will begin to experience

THE BLACK WOMAN'S BODY IMAGE DIET

new intrinsic motivations, so allow this list to be ongoing. Keep it in your Body Positive Living journal and refer to it often, especially during those times when you need to remind yourself just how great you're going to feel after your next joyful movement session.

Step Six

EATING FEEL-GOOD FOODS

I remember how my grandmother used to make the most delicious bacon sandwiches for me when I had to stay home from school because I was sick. They were super thin, so yummy, and made with such love that I actually looked forward to sick days. To this day, I can get a whiff of bacon cooking and be immediately teleported back to those days with my grandmother and her skinny bacon sandwiches. It's amazing how just the smell of a particular food can elicit very specific memories. Food is powerful.

I'm willing to bet that food and eating are at the center of some of your most memorable moments. Sitting around the dinner table sharing stories with your family over Big Mama's fried chicken, mac 'n cheese, candied yams, and collards. Falling in love with your spouse over candlelight dinners. Baking Christmas cookies with your kids. We all have so many wonderful memories linked to food. Of course, the consumption of food and water in certain amounts is necessary for survival. We need appropriate amounts of carbohydrates,

MELINDA GORE

proteins, fats, vitamins, and minerals to support daily activity, including joyful movement. But food symbolizes so much more than physical nourishment.

Eating can also be a very emotional endeavor for many—even a source of pain. Words like *full*, *satisfied*, *happy*, and *pleased* may often describe how you feel after a delicious meal. Yet words like *bloated*, *irritable*, *lethargic*, *gassy*, *crampy*, *upset*, *tired*, *distracted*, *sleepy*, *nauseated*, *sick*, *guilty*, *hungry*, *regretful*, and *stuffed* are just a few other words that may describe how you sometimes feel after eating as well. Some of the words are positive, yet others are negative. Some describe psychological feelings while others describe physiological symptoms. Let's take a closer look at how food makes us feel and how the selection of certain foods can lead to increased feelings of joy and well-being. This leads us to the sixth step toward body positive living, which is becoming more aware of what feel-good foods are and how they may impact the way you see and feel about your body.

EATING FOR HEALTH, NOT WEIGHT LOSS

Don't fret. Nothing has changed now that we've plunged into a food discussion. Just as before, the focus here is not weight loss. Instead, the goal is to highlight how the foods we eat make us feel, both physically and emotionally. Granted, much of the research on the role of food in body image has to do with eating disorders, and eating disorders are not just a "white

THE BLACK WOMAN'S BODY IMAGE DIET

girl's sickness." They affect Black women too and are serious illnesses that require specialized attention and treatment.[114] However, that is not what we are talking about here. Nor are we talking about reducing obesity, even though non-Hispanic Black women in the U.S. suffer disproportionately from obesity and the chronic health diseases associated with it.[115] The good news, though, is that many of the healthy eating habits we're going to discuss can lead to weight improvements and, more important, better health.

So we will focus on making more informed choices when it comes to food and not eating specifically for the sake of weight loss. My goal with this important topic is to encourage you to incorporate a variety of feel-good foods into your current eating plan. I also hope that you find new foods to enjoy and, at your own pace, begin to replace some less healthy foods with better options more frequently. I'd like to see you eating for health and improved mood because, as you will learn, the better you feel, the better you will feel about your body.

But first, it is important for *you* to acknowledge that there is indeed a connection between the foods you eat and how you feel. Take a few minutes and think back to your most recent Thanksgiving. Remember feeling stuffed when you left the dinner table? Or maybe you avoided feeling stuffed and managed to stop eating when you were pleasantly full. How about the last time you binge-watched your favorite show on Netflix and binged your way through the pantry at the same time? Or maybe when you left the house in the middle of the night in pursuit of whatever snack you were craving that just wouldn't let you sleep? Reflect on moments such as these and recall how you

83

felt, both physically and emotionally. Give words to the feelings. Perhaps write in your Body Positive Living journal about one or two of the episodes. You will realize how much food and eating can affect how you feel.

But *how* do the foods you eat contribute to your body image? Good question. Body confidence means feeling optimistic, secure, and self-assured about your body. Research tells us that healthy eating can help a person's body feel better, which will help improve body confidence over time.[116] You may not realize it, but eating unhealthy foods could be contributing negatively to the way you see your body—not necessarily because of weight gain, but because of how certain foods make your body feel and how they affect your mood.

Earlier, I discussed how challenging it is to trust body image because so many things can trigger changes in our perception of our body at any given moment. Our mood plays a big part in our response to those triggers. Eating feel-good foods is a bit like insurance against those times when the inevitable triggers occur. On the other hand, consuming certain foods can lead to increased agitation and even depression. Research supports that people who regularly eat a lot of sweetened beverages, pastries, and refined sugars have an increased risk of depression.[117] Black women should take heed of this warning since a national survey suggests that we are more likely than White women to report feeling "sad" most of the time or to say that "everything is an effort."[118]

When you find yourself feeling down because of the foods you've eaten, it's easy for that self-critical little voice to show up and make all kinds of suggestions to you about your body. By making food choices that regulate mood and keep those feelings at bay, you may have a better chance of keeping that self-critical little voice quiet. Or at the very least, you are better able to manage it appropriately. In other words, simply by selecting healthy foods, you are proactively doing the work to manage how you see and feel about your body.

It is common knowledge that not getting enough of the right nutrients can keep you from feeling your best. We get our nutrients from a variety of sources. However, evidence shows that people who eat more fruits and vegetables have better mental health. Higher consumption of fruits and vegetables is correlated with several psychological benefits, including a lower incidence of depression and anxiety, greater happiness, higher life satisfaction, and greater social and emotional well-being.[119] You can see why the consumption of feel-good foods is an essential component of body positive living. This practice must become a way of life. Consider it an ongoing treatment plan. Soon taking care of yourself, loving and appreciating yourself, and seeing your body more positively will become a way of life as well.

Now let's dive deeper into what feel-good foods are and learn more about how they impact the way you see and feel about your body.

WHAT ARE FEEL-GOOD FOODS?

Foods qualify as feel-good foods for different reasons. The first reason is that they are generally healthy foods that are good

MELINDA GORE

for us: fresh fruits, vegetables, and lean proteins. The second reason is that they are prepared in a healthy manner. Examples include those that are baked (instead of deep-fried), organic (when possible) and free of artificial additives. But, most importantly, foods qualify as feel-good foods because they actually leave us feeling better—they are mood-boosters.

When I call these foods "mood-boosters," I'm not referring to a deceptive, short-term sensation where you feel great for a little while and then crash only hours later. Recall some of the words we listed at the start of the chapter. Feel-good foods are the ones that evoke more positive physiological and emotional responses than negative ones. The science behind food's ability to affect mood is based on the logic that dietary changes are believed to bring about chemical changes in our brain structure, which can lead to changes in our behavior and emotions.[120] Food does this by affecting the production of neurotransmitters, which are brain chemicals that regulate mood.

But what about the feel-not-so-good foods? I never want to refer to any food as "bad" because I believe you can enjoy a number of foods when you exercise moderation. The feel-not-so-good foods include the usual suspects like sugar, refined carbohydrates, processed foods, and caffeine—especially when consumed in excessive amounts. Foods like sugary sweets, sodas, bagels, muffins, cakes, and cookies can all cause unpleasant changes to your mood. They do this primarily by dumping a load of sugar into the bloodstream, causing blood sugar levels to peak and fall very quickly.

Instead of reaching for these unhealthy mood-busters, select foods containing the following mood-boosting nutrients:

THE BLACK WOMAN'S BODY IMAGE DIET

complex carbohydrates, omega-3 fatty acids, vitamin D, the B vitamins, and the mineral selenium. Many of these nutrients help to reduce anxiety, boost mood, and cause you to feel better and more confident about yourself.[121] Let's take a closer look at each.

> **Carbohydrates.** You have probably heard the terms "good carbs" and "bad carbs." Again, I don't endorse the use of the term "bad" to describe any food, but some carbohydrates simply provide more nutritional bang for your buck than others. Good carbohydrates are the complex carbohydrates. Your body needs them to produce serotonin. Remember those neurotransmitters I spoke about? Serotonin is one of them. It is a brain chemical that regulates mood and has a calming effect. Tryptophan, an amino acid found in most protein-rich foods, actually boosts the synthesis of serotonin in the brain. You boost your tryptophan levels in the brain by eating more of the complex carbohydrates. They help tryptophan to enter the brain more easily. Complex carbohydrates are high in fiber. They include foods like whole wheat pasta, vegetables, oats, brown rice, and whole-grain rye bread.

> **Protein.** Proteins contain the amino acids that the brain converts into neurotransmitters. This is why balanced eating is so important. Great sources of protein include meat, fish, eggs, and low-fat cheese. Getting a healthy combination of carbohydrates and protein working together is key for the greatest mood-boosting impact.

Omega-3 Fatty Acids. Foods rich in omega-3 fatty acids have been shown to boost memory and mood.[122] It appears that omega-3s help to improve pathways for neurotransmitters in the brain. To get the most benefits from omega-3 fatty acids, nutritional experts recommend consuming at least two servings of fatty fish (salmon, mackerel, or sardines) per week. Other good sources include ground flaxseeds and walnuts.

Vitamin D. It is shown that vitamin D also increases the amount of serotonin in the brain.[123] It is possibly one of the most powerful antioxidants, which makes it a very important addition to a well-balanced way of eating. However, we can't rely on food alone for our vitamin D. Spending time in the sun is our greatest source. Actually, mushrooms that have been exposed to sunlight are the best food source of vitamin D. Other foods rich in vitamin D include eggs, yogurt, oily fish, and fortified cereals.

B vitamins. Delicious foods like spinach, avocado, broccoli, lean meat, dairy, and eggs are great sources of the various B vitamins, which are essential for energy production. Insufficient amounts of thiamine or vitamin B1 in the diet are associated with feelings of fatigue, decreased self-confidence, and poor mood.[124] It is important to get enough. Additional sources include cereal grains, cauliflower, and oranges.

Selenium. Research supports a connection between low concentrations of the mineral selenium and poor mood.[125] To combat this effect, include sources of selenium like oysters,

THE BLACK WOMAN'S BODY IMAGE DIET

clams, sardines, freshwater and saltwater fish, nuts and seeds, lean pork and beef, skinless chicken and turkey, whole grains, beans, legumes, and low-fat dairy in your daily meal planning.

Of course, I do not expect you to memorize all the foods that have the potential to boost your mood. Instead, I suggest you make a list of the foods you enjoy that contain these nutrients and gradually add them to your daily eating routine. The good news is that feel-good foods that contain these mood-boosting nutrients are pretty easy to identify. As it turns out, many mood-boosting, feel-good foods are healthy foods as well, so you will find them in many wonderful eating regimens that offer a healthy balance of foods. For instance, consuming a Mediterranean diet rich in olives, nuts, and seeds has proven time and again to be particularly good at promoting health and balanced mood, but there is also Whole 30, The Clean Program, and many other healthy ways of eating that stabilize mood. Maybe you would like to go 100 percent vegan or pescatarian. Maybe you'd like to engage in some sort of annual cleanse. It's your choice. The key is to continue trying new things until you find what works for you.

LET'S COOK!

If you are anything like me, you probably spend hours and hours watching cooking programs on television. I love the way they make the food look so delicious and beautiful and simple to prepare. While I am definitely no Giada De Laurentiis, Carla

MELINDA GORE

Hall, "B" Smith, or Ina Garten, I do enjoy the preparation of a beautiful meal, and I *live* for a good dessert. I especially love a dish that is created with powerful mood-boosting ingredients. On the next few pages, I've included a few recipes featuring ingredients that contain many of those powerful mood-boosting nutrients we just discussed.

But wait! Does this mean you have to give up Big Mama's fried chicken or candied yams? No, indeed. I am not suggesting that every meal you eat or prepare should always include only feel-good foods. As I will explain below, everyone deserves a treat sometimes. Did you know, though, that many traditional soul foods are high in vitamins and nutrients? Take, for instance, collards and yams. The trick is to prepare them in a healthier way. For instance, you can ditch the ham hocks in the collards for smoked, skinless turkey breast or swap out the brown sugar on the yams for cinnamon and a splash of OJ.[126] You can also try oven-fried chicken as an alternative to deep-fried chicken. Want more healthy soul food tips? Nowadays you can find numerous soul food cookbooks and websites that will show you how you can still "throw down" in the kitchen, just in a healthier way.[127]

The following recipes are merely a starting point to get you thinking about ways that you can incorporate mood-boosting foods as a part of body positive living. I am a firm believer that when you do something beneficial for yourself—like reaching for a healthy snack instead of an unhealthy one—it goes a long way in helping you to feel better about your body. You know how the saying goes: "You are what you eat!"

Raw Vegetable Collard Green Wraps with Avocado and Tahini

PREP TIME: 10 MINUTES
COOK TIME: 0 MINUTES
YIELDS: 4 SERVINGS

- 4 collard green leaves, trimmed (directions below)
- 3 carrots, shredded or thinly sliced
- 1/2 small purple cabbage, thinly sliced
- 1 yellow pepper, thinly sliced
- 2 vine-ripe tomatoes, thinly sliced
- 1 ripe avocado, pit removed, peeled, sliced into 8 wedges
- 1 cup arugula micro greens
- 1/4 cup fresh mint, roughly chopped
- 1/2 cup tahini, for serving

To prepare your collard greens:

Trim the stems off the bottom of each collard green. Place the leaves flat side down, and then using a sharp paring knife trim down the excess stem so that it is thin and flat along the leaf. The less stem there is, the easier it will be to roll up (and eat!) the collards. Prepare an ice bath. Fill a large mixing bowl with ice and cold water, then set aside.

Bring a large pot of water to a boil. Place the leaves in the boiling water and cook for about 30 seconds. Immediately submerge

MELINDA GORE

cooked collards in the ice bath and let sit for 5 minutes. Remove each collard leaf and dry well with a paper towel, then lay out on a cutting board, stem side facing up.

Lay your prepared vegetables, micro greens, and mint along the center of each collard green lengthwise, distributing evenly between the 4 wraps and making sure to leave at least 1" on all sides. Drizzle each with about 2 Tbsp of tahini. Fold up the sides of each leaf over the filling, then pull the bottom up over the vegetables and roll up to close each wrap. Using a sharp knife, cut each wrap down the middle on a diagonal. Serve immediately.

Nutrition Facts: Servings: 4
Amount per serving (% Daily Value*)
Calories: 246
Total Fat: 18.1g (23%)
Saturated Fat: 3.1g (16%)
Cholesterol 0mg (0%)
Sodium: 211mg (9%)
Total Carbohydrate: 18.5g (7%)

Dietary Fiber: 7.6g (27%) Total Sugars: 4.9g Protein: 6g
Vitamin D: 0mcg (0%) Calcium: 82mg (6%) Iron:
2mg (11%) Potassium: 671mg (14%)
*Percent Daily Values are based on a 2,000 calorie diet.

THE BLACK WOMAN'S BODY IMAGE DIET

Deviled Eggs with Guacamole and Pickled Onions

PREP TIME: 15 MINUTES

COOK TIME: 11 MINUTES

YIELDS: 12 SERVINGS

For the pickled red onions:

- 1/4 small red onion, thinly sliced
- 1/2 cup rice wine vinegar
- 1 tbsp whole black peppercorns
- 1/4 tsp sugar
- 1/4 tsp salt

For the deviled eggs:

- 12 large eggs
- 4 tbsp mayonnaise (Paleo mayo, if desired)
- 3 tsp Dijon
- 1/2 tsp salt
- pinch of freshly ground black pepper
- 1 tbsp chives, chopped
- paprika, for garnish

For the guacamole:

- 1 avocado, ripe
- 1 tsp salt
- 1/2 lime, juiced
- 2 tbsp cilantro, chopped

MELINDA GORE

To make pickled red onions:

Bring 2 cups of water to a boil, then add sliced red onion and cook for 1 minute. Drain onions, then set aside. In a small container with a lid or a small bowl, combine vinegar, peppercorns, sugar, and salt. Add red onions, then place lid on top and shake. Otherwise stir to combine, cover with plastic wrap, and set in the fridge for at least 1 hour.

To make the deviled eggs:

Place eggs in a single layer in a large pot, then cover with 2-3 inches of water. Bring to a boil, remove from the heat, cover, and let stand for 11 minutes. While eggs are cooking, prepare an ice bath by placing ice in a large bowl and filling most of the way to the top with cold water.

Drain eggs and immediately place in the ice bath to cool. Let sit 5 minutes, then peel gently.

Cut eggs in half lengthwise and carefully pop the yolks out. Place yolks in a large bowl, then mash with the back of a fork. Add mayonnaise, mustard, salt, and pepper, then stir to combine. If the filling is not spreadable, add another tsp of mayonnaise or mustard until desired consistency is reached.

Fill each egg with 1-2 teaspoons of filling, then place in refrigerator to cool for 1 hour.

To make guacamole:

While eggs are cooling, mash avocado with lime juice, salt, and chopped cilantro. When ready, top eggs with a heaping teaspoon of guacamole. Sprinkle on a pinch of paprika, then top with pickled red onions. Enjoy cold or at room temperature.

Nutrition Facts: Servings: 12
Amount per serving (% Daily Value*)
Calories: 149
Total Fat: 12.3g (16%) Saturated Fat: 2.7g (14%)
Cholesterol 193mg (64%) Sodium: 287mg (12%)
Total Carbohydrate: 2.4g (1%) Dietary Fiber: 1.2g (4%)
Total Sugars: 0.7g Protein: 6.7g
Vitamin D: 18mcg (88%) Calcium: 30mg (2%)
Iron: 1mg (6%) Potassium: 155mg (3%)

Shredded Asian Chicken Slaw

PREP TIME: 15 MINUTES
COOK TIME: 0 MINUTES
YIELDS: 8 SERVINGS

For the dressing:

- 1/4 cup grape seed oil
- 2 tbsp rice wine vinegar
- 1 tbsp honey
- 1 tsp sesame oil
- 1/2 tsp Sriracha (optional)
- Juice of 2 limes (about 3 tbsp)
- 1 tsp kosher salt
- 1/4 tsp freshly ground black pepper

For the slaw:

- 1/2 store-bought rotisserie chicken, shredded
- 4 cups prepared shredded cabbage or coleslaw
- 2 cups prepared shredded carrots
- 4 radishes, shredded
- 1 red bell pepper, thinly sliced and cut into bite-size pieces
- 1 mango, ripe but firm
- 1 cup edamame, shelled and cooked
- 1/2 cup scallions, thinly sliced (about 2 scallions)
- 1/4 cup raw cashew halves
- 1 tbsp sesame seeds
- Fresh cilantro, for garnish

To make the dressing:

Combine grape seed oil, vinegar, honey, lime juice, Sriracha (optional), salt, and pepper in a glass jar with lid. Shake until well mixed, then set aside.

To make the slaw:

Peel mango with a vegetable peeler, then slice into thin strips about the same size as the other vegetables. Combine chicken, cabbage, carrots, radishes, bell pepper, mango, edamame, scallions, and cashews in a large bowl. Pour dressing on top, then gently toss to combine. Let sit for at least 15 minutes to allow the vegetables to soak up the dressing, but 1 hour is better. Serve room temperature or cold. Garnish with toasted sesame seeds and fresh cilantro.

Nutrition Facts: Servings: 8
Amount per serving (% Daily Value*)
Calories: 243
Total Fat: 13.7g (18%)
Saturated Fat: 1.9g (9%)
Cholesterol 16mg (5%)
Sodium: 342mg (15%)
Total Carbohydrate: 21.1g (8%)

Dietary Fiber: 4.3g (15%) Total Sugars: 11.7g Protein: 11.4g
Vitamin D: 0mcg (0%) Calcium: 115mg (9%) Iron:
2mg (13%) Potassium: 557mg (12%)

MELINDA GORE

Warm Chopped Brussels Sprouts Salad with Roasted Chicken

PREP TIME: 15 MINUTES
COOK TIME: < 10 MINUTES
YIELDS: 6 SERVINGS

For the dressing:

- 1/2 cup olive oil
- 3 tbsp apple cider vinegar
- 1 shallot, minced
- 2 tsp fresh rosemary, chopped
- 1 tsp Dijon
- 1 tsp salt

For the salad:

- 1 1/2 lbs Brussels sprouts, ends trimmed
- 2 tbsp grapeseed oil
- 1/2 tsp salt
- 1/4 tsp pepper
- juice from 1/2 an orange
- 1/4 cup pumpkin seeds
- 1/4 tsp cinnamon
- pinch of cayenne
- 1/2 store-bought rotisserie chicken, meat pulled
- 3 oz Manchego cheese

To make the dressing:

Combine dressing ingredients in a mason jar fitted with a lid. Shake until well mixed, then set aside.

To make the salad:

Cut each Brussels sprout in half lengthwise, then lay flat on a cutting board. Use a sharp knife to thinly slice until all Brussels are shredded.

Preheat oil in a large skillet over medium-high heat. When hot, add Brussels sprouts and cook, stirring often, about 5 minutes, or until tender. Season with salt and pepper, then squeeze juice from half an orange directly on top. Cook for 1 minute more, then remove and place in a large bowl.

Heat a small non-stick skillet over medium heat, then add pumpkin seeds, cinnamon, and a pinch of cayenne. Cook, stirring often, until pumpkin seeds are lightly browned and fragrant, about 2 minutes.

Add pumpkin seeds, rotisserie chicken, and Manchego cheese to the Brussels sprouts. Pour dressing on top, toss to combine, then serve immediately.

MELINDA GORE

Nutrition Facts: Servings: 6
Amount per serving (% Daily Value*)
Calories: 317
Total Fat: 26.2g (34%)
Saturated Fat: 4g (20%)
Cholesterol 21mg (7%)
Sodium: 641mg (28%)
Total Carbohydrate: 13g (5%)

Dietary Fiber: 4.8g (17%) Total Sugars: 3g Protein: 12.2g
Vitamin D: 0mcg (0%) Calcium: 54mg (4%) Iron:
3mg (16%) Potassium: 578mg (12%)

Muffins with Coconut Yogurt, Fresh Berries, and Honey

PREP TIME: 5 MINUTES
COOK TIME: 25 MINUTES
YIELDS: 12 MUFFINS

- 2 cups Paleo baking flour (such as Bob's Red Mill)
- 1/2 cup pecans, finely ground
- 1 tsp cinnamon
- 1 tsp baking soda
- 1/2 tsp kosher salt
- 1/3 cup coconut oil, melted and cooled 1/4 cup pure maple syrup
- 3 large eggs, room temperature
- 1 tsp vanilla extract
- Coconut oil spray
- 1 cup coconut yogurt
- Fresh blueberries
- Honey, for drizzling

Preheat oven to 350°F. Line a standard-sized muffin tin with muffin liners, then grease with coconut oil spray.

In a large bowl, whisk together Paleo baking flour, ground pecans, cinnamon, baking soda, and salt, then set aside.

In a separate small bowl, whisk together coconut oil, maple syrup, eggs, and vanilla extract. Pour in flour mixture and stir until just combined. Use a standard size cookie scoop to portion batter evenly and place into prepared cups. Press down slightly on the top to form a flat base (this will help hold the yogurt and toppings!).

Bake 20-25 minutes, or until a toothpick inserted in the center of the muffin comes out clean. Cool muffins in pan for 5 minutes, then transfer to a wire rack to finish cooling.

Top each muffin with a dollop of coconut yogurt, then place about 1 Tbsp of fresh berries on top, and drizzle with honey. Serve immediately.

Nutrition Facts: Servings: 12
Amount per serving (% Daily Value*)
Calories: 213
Total Fat: 12.2g (16%)
Saturated Fat: 8.8g (44%)
Cholesterol 48mg (16%)
Sodium: 264mg (11%)
Total Carbohydrate: 20.8g (8%)

Dietary Fiber: 7.2g (26%) Total Sugars: 10g Protein: 5.6g
Vitamin D: 4mcg (22%) Calcium: 27mg (2%) Iron: 3mg (16%) Potassium: 48mg (1%)

Crunchy Chocolate Nut Bars with Toasted Coconut

PREP TIME: 10 MINUTES
COOK TIME: 30 MINUTES
YIELDS: 9 SERVINGS

- 3⁄4 cup walnuts
- 3⁄4 cup almonds
- 1⁄4 cup Paleo baking flour (such as Bob's Red Mill)
- 1⁄2 tsp kosher salt
- 1⁄4 cup maple syrup or honey
- 2 egg whites
- 1 tsp vanilla extract
- 1 tbsp toasted coconut flakes
- 2 tbsp sliced almonds
- 1⁄4 cup dark chocolate, chopped, plus 3 tbsp more for topping (or drizzle with almond butter)
- 1 tsp Maldon sea salt

Preheat oven to 325°F. Line an 8x8 pan with parchment, then grease with oil spray or baking spray. Add walnuts and almonds to a food processor. Process until the nuts resemble a fine crumb.

In a large bowl, combine ground nuts, Paleo flour, and salt, then mix well. Add in maple syrup or honey, egg whites, vanilla, coconut, almonds, and 1⁄4 cup chopped chocolate.

Use a rubber spatula and stir to combine, then pour into prepared pan. Use the spatula to evenly spread the batter and smooth out the top, then bake for 25 minutes, or until golden brown on top. Add remaining chopped chocolate, then cook 3-5 minutes more. Immediately sprinkle with Maldon sea salt. Let bars cool 10 minutes in pan before transferring to a wire rack. Cool completely before slicing into 9 squares.

Nutrition Facts: Servings: 9
Amount per serving (% Daily Value*)
Calories: 242
Total Fat: 15.3g (20%)
Saturated Fat: 4g (20%)
Cholesterol: 1mg (0%)
Sodium: 428mg (19%)
Total Carbohydrate: 20.2g (7%)
Dietary Fiber: 6.7g (24%)
Total Sugars: 10g
Protein: 7.8g
Vitamin D: 0mcg (0%)
Calcium: 53mg (4%)
Iron: 3mg (15%)
Potassium: 188mg (4%)

Now that you have a few delicious, healthy, mood-boosting recipes that you can pull from anytime you want, I encourage you to add your own special touch and preferences and come up with a few of your own. Look online, flip through cookbooks, catch a few cooking shows on television, or try a few from this chapter. Find at least three new recipes made with feel-good foods to add to your routine in the upcoming weeks. Additionally, explore exciting kitchen tools, such as air fryers, high-speed blenders, juicers and mixers that make meal prep healthier and fun.

TIPS FOR FEEL-GOOD EATING

Next, let's consider the behavioral side of feel-good foods. For the rest of the chapter, my goal is to help you put into practice a few principles for eating and enjoying feel-good foods.

As you can see from the dessert recipes included in this chapter, I believe it is perfectly okay to have treats. Treats can be mood-lifting, and they are definitely a part of feel-good eating, but as with anything else, moderation is key, and boundaries are helpful. Take a look at the tips outlined below and adopt what works for you.

> **Clean out the cabinets.** Get rid of all the stuff in your pantry that you know is not good for you and does not move you toward seeing your body more positively. Doing so sets you up for a fighting chance against the cravings. I understand you may want to have ice cream from time to time, and I believe you should be able to—perhaps not every day, but once in a while, for sure. Whenever you do want ice cream, I recommend that you avoid bringing home the half gallon or pint from the grocery store while promising yourself that you'll have only one serving. Don't tempt yourself. Instead, go to your local ice creamery, order a single scoop, and enjoy.

MELINDA GORE

Savor your treats. When you make the decision to partake of a delicious treat, take your time and enjoy it. Instead of mindlessly tearing through a bag of Hershey's Kisses only to be left with a sick tummy, a mountain of silver wrappers, and disappointment when you reach into the empty bag, set aside just a few pieces and put the rest away. Enjoy each Kiss one by one. Open the wrapper slowly, observe its intricate packaging, inhale the wonderful smell of chocolate, and place it on your tongue. Notice how the texture and taste change as the candy melts in your mouth. Slowly and deliberately, savor the chocolatey goodness between your teeth, noticing its distinct flavor, and truly allow yourself a moment to enjoy. Maybe you won't do this every time you eat, but I urge you to give the method a try with all of your special treats. Take time to enjoy them. No more mindless eating.

Monitor serving sizes. Become more aware of serving sizes and make it a habit to read the label on the foods you eat. You will notice far less of that full, bloated feeling when you stick to the suggested serving size. Additionally, you may try selecting a smaller dinner plate until you get used to seeing less food on your plate. Whatever foods you choose, as often as you can, eat from a dish rather than the package. Taking the time to place your serving in a dish really helps improve your awareness of what and how much you are eating.

Adopt a regular eating schedule. Eating regularly is great for the metabolism and helps you avoid the dangers that can arise when you skip meals. It helps to stabilize your mood.

THE BLACK WOMAN'S BODY IMAGE DIET

Especially make sure you eat breakfast. If your mother insisted that you eat breakfast, she had the right idea. Breakfast is the most important meal of the day when it comes to regulating your mood. According to research, people who eat breakfast regularly have better memory and experience more feelings of calmness, and their mood and energy levels are more consistent throughout the day.[128] A high-fiber breakfast, like oatmeal with fresh berries, makes a great choice. Also, take your time when eating a meal; do it at the table without distractions. It takes approximately 30 minutes for the feeling of fullness to set in. Give your body time to feel full instead of scarfing down your food before your body has a chance. Speaking of fullness, make sure you are full after dinner so that you won't be tempted to raid the kitchen or order munchies late at night. Not only can late-night snacking put extra pounds on you, but it also can disrupt your sleep and put you at greater risk of developing diabetes and heart disease. Clearly, none of these outcomes will make you feel better about your body. So, if you are a late-night snacker, try eating within an earlier window of time, for instance, between 8 a.m. and 8 p.m. Such "intermittent fasting" may even decrease your blood sugar, cholesterol, inflammation, and body fat.[129]

Limit the usual suspects. Your body can do without the peaks and valleys brought on by added sugar. As mentioned earlier, cutting down on sugar can help you feel better about yourself as well. In general, fried foods are not your friend. Baking or air frying is always a better option than traditional frying, but moderation is key. Remember this body image diet is not about weight loss or strict rules. It is about taking care of yourself and beginning to feel better about how you see yourself in the process. Doing good things for your body goes a long way.

Limit processed foods. Just a quick note about processed foods. In an effort to thwart the shifts in mood that may trigger your self-critical little voice, avoiding heavily processed foods is key. We've already spoken about sugar, but many processed foods contain ungodly amounts of salt, sugar, white flour and preservatives. Rather than reaching for packaged cookies, chips and items that try to pass as healthy, like granola bars and protein bars (be sure to read the labels), have fresh fruit, mixed nuts, or vegetables and hummus instead. Research tells us that not only do these healthier food choices play a vital role in improving our mood, but also help to reduce stress and even lower our risk for dementia.[130]

Create a weekly meal plan. I'm sure you've heard it before, but creating a meal plan for the week can help you to stay on track. Once you determine which feel-good foods you prefer, incorporate them into your weekly meal plan. Getting organized will assist you greatly in reaching your goals. You're adding new foods and recipes to your routine, so set aside a day to do the grocery shopping. As soon as you get home, wash your fresh fruits and vegetables and place them in easy-to-access containers. But cut yourself some slack. Rome was not built in a day. You'll get the hang of it. The more you do it, the more efficient you'll become.

Embrace variety. Not only is variety the spice of life, but it's the key to preventing boredom. It's always a good idea to incorporate a variety of foods into your daily menu. It allows for optimal exposure to vitamins and minerals. Strive to eat a colorful rainbow of fruits and vegetables. It's a great way to ensure you're getting all those beneficial nutrients. Also, incorporating gluten-free grains into your diet like oats, buckwheat, quinoa and millet is a great way to mix things up as well.

Drink up. Don't forget about water. Hydration is key. Our bodies need water. Did you know that our muscles are 75 percent water?[131] Strong muscles equate to strong bodies. If you know you are not a big water drinker, come up with creative ways to get more water into your body each day. For example, if you drink colas and sugary drinks, try serving them over full glasses of ice as a way to wean yourself off them and find a healthy replacement. It also helps to keep a water bottle at your side throughout the day. Make sure you're getting enough water. Aim for at least 64 ounces per day and more if you are really active.

MELINDA GORE

BODY IMAGE BOOSTER: FOOD AND MOOD JOURNAL

There really is only one reliable way to determine how foods impact your mood and that is by keeping a food journal. This is not about counting calories or restricting your food intake, but about creating awareness.

This week, I would like you to keep a food and mood journal of everything you eat for three consecutive days. Document your emotions as well as how you feel physically before, during, and after each meal. Notice whether you experience changes in mood and, if so, whether they are positive or negative. Increased awareness can guide you in making the best possible food choices. It may also be a good idea to monitor what you have eaten those times when you find yourself tuning in to critical thoughts about your body as well.

*Please visit www.freegiftfrommelinda.com
for printable worksheets to guide you through
each chapter's Body Image Booster.*

PART III

RE-INVIGORATING YOUR SPIRIT

Step Seven

EXPRESS YOUR SPIRITUALITY

Now that we've considered the importance of feeding your body with feel-good foods to promote body positive living, let's talk about feeding your spirit to do the same. A number of studies over the years have demonstrated a link between spiritual well-being and improved physical health. Spirituality is also associated with a more positive outlook and better quality of life.[132] I think we can all agree that body positive living is consistent with all three: improved physical health, positive outlook, and better quality of life. For these reasons, it is essential that we discuss the seventh step toward body positive living, which involves expressing your spirituality through prayer, meditation, and journaling, while embracing the positive impact each has on the way you see and feel about your body.

It is important to note that spirituality should not be confused with religion. Rather, it is a measure of self-care. Spirituality has the potential to affect many aspects of your life, including giving it a sense of meaning, being at peace with yourself, enhancing the ability to engage in compassionate and giving relationships, as well as the ability to practice forgiveness—all of which are strongly related to positive health outcomes.[133] One study found that greater spiritual well-being was associated with significantly lower inflammation in the body, lower blood sugar, and lower blood pressure.[134] It's studies like this one that demonstrate the value of incorporating spirituality into your daily way of living. For Black women in particular, spirituality has significant value since, as I noted earlier, Black women suffer from diabetes and hypertension at disproportionate rates.

Spirituality is a broad topic that leaves a lot of room for many perspectives. You will notice throughout this chapter that I am sharing my personal experiences and relationship with God. However, I am not suggesting that your relationship with God or your higher power must look exactly like mine. Instead, I simply feel it is important to give you a personal example of spirituality. That said, allow me to explain what spirituality means to me and why I have included prayer, meditation, and journaling as important components of *The Black Woman's Body Image Diet*.

DEFINING SPIRITUALITY

Merriam-Webster defines *well-being* as the state of being happy, healthy, or prosperous.[135] A more inclusive definition comes from WellCoaches Inc., which tells us that well-being is not simply the absence of disease but instead the culmination of all the behaviors that lead to total health and wellness.[136]

THE BLACK WOMAN'S BODY IMAGE DIET

While most dictionaries offer similar definitions for the word *well-being*, the term *spiritual well-being* is not so easily defined. Because we already have a working definition of well-being, let's begin by gaining a deeper understanding of spirituality. First and foremost, spirituality means different things to different people. The National Cancer Institute defines spirituality as deep religious feelings and beliefs, including a person's sense of peace, purpose, connection to others, and beliefs about the meaning of life.[137] The National Institute of Healthcare Research describes it as the feelings, thoughts, experiences, and behaviors that arise from a search for the sacred.[138] Others say it is an internal process of seeking personal authenticity, genuineness, and wholeness as an aspect of identity development.[139]

Despite the variety of definitions, I believe we can agree that spirituality is a journey and not a destination. For me, spirituality can be defined only by the truth it is based upon. It describes my relationship with God—my connectedness to God. It is the expression of my day-to-day, moment-by-moment trust and reliance on Him. Therefore, for the purpose of this book, *spirituality* will describe a person's connectedness to God, and *spiritual well-being* will describe the culmination of all the behaviors that contribute to a healthy, prosperous connectedness to God.

Before we go any further, I want to acknowledge that you may have beliefs that are different from mine. I approach my spirituality from the perspective of my faith as a Christian, and that is how I've framed many of the suggestions you will find in this chapter. Whether you hold the same views or not, you can still practice prayer, meditation, and journaling. You should

MELINDA GORE

simply tap into whatever gives you strength and clarity when you feel overwhelmed or need guidance.

We've already spoken about the power of positive self-talk. If you don't want to pray to God or meditate on a Bible verse as I will suggest, you can instead work on your positive self-talk. Of course, you also have the option to skip this section of the program, but I hope you won't because you will miss an important step. It's important because the primary goal for re-invigorating your spirituality is to develop practices that will equip you to feel more positively about your body and to resist the temptation to listen to negative thoughts.

SPIRITUAL EXPRESSION

While this program emphasizes caring for your mind, body, and spirit, spirituality is the foundation that everything is built upon—balanced health, well-being in every area of your life, and especially body positive living. Your spirit, which is your inner being, is the deepest part of yourself. Through the spirit we connect and commune with God. Therefore, to express your spirituality is to express your connectedness to God.

As Black women, we wear many hats. Especially, as we enter middle-age, we are often tasked with taking care of children, spouses, parents, and a job (or business) as well as ourselves. On top of that, we must cope with the stress of living in a society where we expect to encounter racism and sexism every day. In spite of these challenges, too many of us try to live up to the stereotype of "The Strong Black Woman," a resilient,

THE BLACK WOMAN'S BODY IMAGE DIET

emotionally contained, self-sacrificing superwoman who can do it all![140] However, to practice the art of body positive living, we must put systems in place that allow us to rest, refresh, and refuel. Spending quiet time alone with God, on a regular basis, helps us to accomplish this and express our spirituality. As we move forward, we will explore the multitude of benefits associated with expressing your spirituality and taking the time to rest, refresh, and refuel.

So, what does any of this have to do with body positive living? Well, everything, if you ask me. A great deal of research reveals that spiritual well-being and belief in a higher power both have a positive impact on body image. Women who feel loved and accepted by God experience reduced levels of risk for eating disorders, are buffered from exposure to thin-ideal media, report higher levels of positive body image, and engage in body-related comparisons less frequently.[141] Specifically, research finds that belief in the sanctity of your body, belief in the role of God in creating your body, and trust in God or your higher power's partnership during times of stress are all associated with increased body satisfaction.[142] So the expression of your spirituality through practices like prayer, meditation, and journaling not only allow for quiet time for resting, refreshing, and refueling, but the cultivation of positive body image as well.

No matter how you have expressed your spirituality in the past, finding new ways to calm the chaos of life, quiet your mind, and connect with God is key. Regularly spending time alone and finding calm and peace are necessary for your well-being and body positive living. Through these practices, your experience of God's love grows. Through God's Word you come to understand truth and begin to believe that you are accepted. Doing so will allow you to tap into your spirituality on your journey to body positive living.

By the time you finish this chapter, you will be equipped with effective tools to help you find the truth amidst the multitude of negative thoughts and messages that may tempt you to feel negatively about your body. Let's get acquainted with prayer, meditation, and journaling.

PRAYER

As we have discussed, you most likely feel overwhelmed by the bombardment of messages regarding your body. In addition to being overwhelmed by the messages, you may feel pulled in ten different directions just to accomplish all the many requisite tasks you have in a day. During those times when everyone and everything seem to be speaking to you so loudly, quiet time spent in prayer may allow you to center yourself, regain clarity, and face the day.

Prayer is a powerful thing. Prayer does not have to be complicated and confusing, nor does it need to be deep. It is basically spending one-on-one time in the presence of God. For me, prayer is time spent conversing with God. It does not always involve asking for anything; it is sometimes simply a time to listen, receive direction, and give thanks.

The good news is that you can pray anywhere. In the car, at the gym, or even while having your teeth cleaned. One of

THE BLACK WOMAN'S BODY IMAGE DIET

my favorite times to pray is during long walks on the beach. Looking out at the beauty and massiveness of the ocean always reminds me of just how small I am and just how big He is. In general, spending time outside appreciating nature is a way I am able to quiet the noise and spend time with God. You may try listening to motivational messages or inspirational music for encouragement, or you might search online for other ideas. Developing a prayer life is not about rules; it's about cultivating a relationship with God.

Prayer has proven to be an effective coping mechanism to deal with body image and eating concerns.[143] Research also shows that praying more, having a closer relationship with God, and having higher intrinsic religious orientation is related to feeling better about your weight and appearance.[144]

As a Christian, I know that just because negative messages are out there, I shouldn't assume that they are for me. It is my quiet time alone with God in prayer that helps me to remember who I am and whose I am. I am God's child. When I find myself believing what the world says about me more than what God says about me, I know that things are off and my focus is on the world, not on God's Word.

God hears us when we pray. When you are feeling overwhelmed with negative thoughts about your body or anything for that matter, pray. When these situations arise, I go straight to God and tell Him just how I'm feeling at the moment. I confidently pour my heart out to Him, just as I would to a dear friend. Once I share my feelings, I then recall what His Word says about my specific concerns. By the end of my prayer, I am uplifted and encouraged. I physically feel refreshed and refueled.

I encourage you to see yourself as God sees you. Spend quiet time in prayer to remind yourself of the truth rather than being pushed around by the lies. A foundational scripture that helps me to keep things in perspective is: "Do not conform any longer to the pattern of this world, but be transformed by the renewing of your mind" (Romans 12:2 NIV). Prayer, according to the Word of God, renews your mind. I repeat: I am not saying that negative messages will never impact you. But regular appointments with God in prayer can help you get back on track when you get off track. When I contemplate His Word, it helps me to replace negative messages, gain hope, and feel empowered to carry on. Believing in something greater than yourself is truly powerful.

MEDITATION

Another way to express your spirituality is through meditation. Meditation is a bit like prayer, but instead of being conversational or listening quietly, you select a single thought or sound as your focus. If you select a thought, you may choose to repeat it out loud, quietly to yourself, or under your breath.

Meditation builds your faith. According to God's Word, "Faith is the substance of things hoped for, the evidence of things not seen" (Hebrews 11:1 NKJV). Having faith means you feel hopeful for things to come. To build faith during meditation, I suggest that you select a scripture related to whatever challenge you may be facing, but you can use any positive thought that motivates you.

Another favorite scripture of mine is: "I praise you because I am fearfully and wonderfully made; your works are wonderful, I know that full well" (Psalm 139:14). I repeat it to myself over and over and allow it to resonate with my spirit when I am struggling with how I see myself and my body. I am reminded that God made me exactly as I am and that there is no need to fret because I am handcrafted by God Himself. It's as if I am depositing the words deep inside. You can do the same. Find a scripture or positive thought and ruminate on it until it becomes your truth.

Rumination is a word used in psychology to describe the act of rehearsing thoughts about whatever is distressing you. It is equated with worry. It's kind of like a short commercial repeating on a loop in your head. However, *rumination* also means "to engage in contemplation." As you may have guessed, the root word of *rumination* is *ruminate*. To ruminate is to chew repeatedly for an extended period. Animals called "ruminants" (cows, for example) must chew their cud to digest their food. They eat grass or hay, swallow it, and later regurgitate it to chew on it again. They do this multiple times to extract all the nutrients from the food.

I bet you're wondering where I'm going with this line of thought. Well, bear with me a little while longer. You see, I once listened to a motivational message delivered by a pastor who beautifully explained that the way cows regurgitate and chew food—or ruminate—is a lot like what we as humans should do in meditation. The idea is to select a positive thought that you would like to meditate on. (Selecting the positive thought is the most important part.) Chew on it. Ponder it. Get it in your spirit. Extract everything from it that you can. Remind yourself what it says. Swallow it and then bring it back up later in your mind. Reflect on what you are saying. Do this often. After a while, the positive messages running on a loop in your head will replace the negative ones—the ones that can cause you to feel bad about your body or anything else. The key is taking the time to engage in this highly beneficial practice.

Many people believe that our thoughts about ourselves dictate who we become. There is a scripture that confirms this principle: "As a man thinketh in his heart, so is he" (Proverbs 23:7). These are wise words. Research shows that reading theistic-religious affirmations about your body can actually improve how you feel about your appearance. Affirmations are positive assertions, and those that emphasize God's embrace of your body as whole—perfect as it is created and deserving of respect—are most effective.[145] I encourage you to express your spirituality by meditating or ruminating on such affirmations. In the "Body Image Booster" exercise at the end of this chapter, you will find more of my favorite affirmations from the Bible. However, take some time to find your favorites, whether they are from sacred texts like the Bible, philosophical books like Kahlil Gibran's The Prophet, or a 12-step program like Overeaters Anonymous. Or create your own affirmations to reinforce positive feelings about yourself.

JOURNALING

As I hope you have experienced by now, journaling is an effective tool to get your thoughts out of your head and down on paper. It can be therapeutic. Additionally, journaling is another great way to express your spirituality. Journaling exercises are included throughout *The Black Woman's Body Image Diet* because they allow you to explore your thoughts and feelings.

We spoke about your vision for a positive body image in the introduction to this book. Journaling provides an excellent opportunity to write your vision down. Is there something in your heart that you've been asking, praying, or believing in God for? Work through it in your journal. You can even try writing your prayers down. However, remember that journaling does not have to be limited to writing words on paper. Previously, I encouraged you to get creative with your Body Positive Living journal: to clip pictures from magazines, draw your own pictures, color on the pages, and include photos of yourself. So, if you wish, make a collage. Add pictures of inspiration. You will soon see the difference it makes in how you see yourself.

The joy of journaling is that it can be whatever you want it to be. Whatever is in your head and heart shows up on paper and eventually shows up in your life. My favorite part of journaling is coming back to entries that I wrote months or even years earlier to remind myself of answered prayers. Also, it allows me to see how much I've grown or to remind myself of places where I still feel a bit stuck. Either way, it heightens my awareness in a positive way, which contributes to how I see myself.

MELINDA GORE

GETTING STARTED

Expressing your spirituality may be a brand-new experience for you. Prayer, meditation, or journaling may be brand-new to you as well, but don't be discouraged. Just start somewhere. Begin by setting aside time in your day to engage in a spiritual expression of your choosing. The three activities outlined in this chapter are not your only options. Your spirituality may be expressed in a number of ways. Taking a yoga class, walking outside in nature, praise dancing, listening to choral or gospel music, singing hymns, and playing an instrument are all examples. Don't be hard on yourself; doing it regularly takes practice. As with any new skill, you'll get better and better. The more time you spend praying, meditating, or journaling, the more you will discover your value is determined by how God sees you, and not anyone else.

BODY IMAGE BOOSTER: AFFIRMATIONS FOR BODY POSITIVE LIVING

Set aside time to explore your own experience with spirituality. I have provided you with many definitions, but what does *spiritual well-being* mean to you? In what ways can your spirituality move you closer to body positive living? Read through scriptures that describe who you are and God's love for you or find affirmations from other sources that speak to your soul. I

THE BLACK WOMAN'S BODY IMAGE DIET

want you to pick out a few of your favorites and remember just how much you are loved every time that self-critical little voice about your body enters your mind. Once you have your favorites, add them to your Body Positive Living journal, and you'll always have them when you need them. I am providing a few below, but I encourage you to find even more.

— I am a child of God. (Romans 8:16)

— I can do everything through Him who gives me strength. (Philippians 4:13)

— Peace I leave with you; my peace I give you. I do not give to you as the world gives. Do not let your heart be troubled and do not be afraid. (John 14:27)

— For we are God's workmanship, created in Christ Jesus to do good works, which God prepared in advance for us to do. (Ephesians 2:10)

— Therefore, there is now no more condemnation for those who are in Christ Jesus. (Romans 8:1)

— Therefore, if anyone is in Christ, he is a new creation; the old has gone, the new has come. (2 Corinthians 5:17)

— And we know that all things work together for good to them that love God, to them who are called according to his purpose. (Romans 8:28)

MELINDA GORE

— Know he not that ye are the temple of God, and that the Spirit of God dwells in you. (1 Corinthians 3:16)

— Do not conform any longer to the pattern of this world, but be transformed by the renewing of your mind. (Romans 12:2)

— The Lord does not look at the things man looks at. Man looks at your outward appearance, but God looks at the heart. (1 Samuel 16:7)

— Cast all your anxiety on Him because He cares for you. (1 Peter 5:7)

Step Eight

KEEP YOUR FRIENDS CLOSE AND THOSE WHO ENCOURAGE YOU CLOSER

On at least a few occasions, when I was much younger, my mother expressed disapproval of my friends. You know how it goes. You're young and naïve, and you desperately feel the need to fit in. She would say, "Mind the company you keep, Melinda, because they are more likely to rub off on you than the other way around." Well, hindsight is 20/20. As I got older, I realized that my mother was right, as was often the case. I watched from a distance as many of those former friends took very different turns in life than I did, all because of the company they chose to keep.

Of course, I am able to say this now, but I am quite sure I was humming a very different tune back then. Today, I totally get it. I fully understand the importance of being discerning about who you choose to surround yourself with. That's why the eighth step toward body positive living requires becoming

MELINDA GORE

selective about the people you allow in your social circle and learning how your friends and associates may impact the way you see and feel about your body.

MIND THE COMPANY YOU KEEP

Social environment plays a major role in human development. The old nature-versus-nurture debate is stronger than ever, but many people agree that a person's environment plays just as great a role in who they become as their genetic makeup. Sure, DNA plays a part, but our social interactions greatly impact the person we become. And that phenomenon doesn't stop when we reach maturity.

Scientists have for many years acknowledged an association between social relationships and health. Individuals who are less socially integrated are less healthy, both psychologically and physically. Believe it or not, the research suggests that lack of social relationships is as much of a health risk as cigarette smoking, high blood pressure, high cholesterol, obesity, and lack of physical activity.[146] While it is important to have social relationships, what may be most important is the quality of such relationships.

Over the course of your life, you've probably found yourself a part of many different social circles. From grade school to college and then in the real world, you became a part of a variety of social networks: from close-knit unions with family and friends to church groups, sororities, sports teams, clubs, coworkers, and, for Black women in particular, even beauty

132

salons. Hopefully, these networks have challenged you to grow and change for the better. Just as it is important to care for your body and your internal environment (your mind and spirit), you also have to nurture your social environment. Doing so boils down to keeping your friends close but keeping those who encourage and uplift you closer.

As women, we place a great deal of importance on our friendships. By the time we reach our thirties, forties, and beyond, we have probably developed sturdy bonds with other women. Many of these bonds may be as strong, if not stronger, than family bonds. Do you agree? Our "girlfriendships" are where we invest a lot of our time and energy. Girlfriends can become like extended family, whether we call them our "sorors," "homegirls," "BFF," or "boo." We do everything together. We throw birthday parties and baby showers and spend time in each other's homes. Accordingly, we must be careful to make sure that these relationships are working *for* us and not against us.

Managing our friendships is so important for us at this stage in our lives. Our friendships should be places of solace and safety—as should all our close relationships. You should walk away from the times spent with friends feeling encouraged and inspired, not depleted or torn down. Above all, hurt feelings or criticism, just for the sake of inflicting pain, should never be tolerated within friendships. As unfortunate as it may sound, there are relationships out there, under the guise of friendship, where these types of behaviors take place. And these behaviors can have a devastating impact on body image.

An increasing amount of research is being conducted in the area of social circles and their impact on body image.

MELINDA GORE

Remember what we said at Step Three about the pitfalls of comparisons and how they may contribute to negative feelings about our bodies? Well, a recent study revealed that appearance-related comparisons with same-sex close friends influence a woman's body image. In the study, whether the comparisons caused friends to feel better about their bodies or worse was determined by how comfortable with intimacy the friends were. Women who avoided intimacy within friendships tended to compare the differences between their physical appearance and the physical appearance of their friends, causing them to feel worse about their bodies. On the other hand, women who were comfortable with intimacy within their friendships, made these types of comparisons far less, allowing them to feel better about their bodies.[147]

As confirmed by this study, women who are immersed in truly close, loving, respectful relationships may not only enrich relationships by helping their friends improve body image, but they also experience a more positive body image themselves.[148] This begs the question: How enriching are your friendships? With all the effort you are putting toward creating a body positive way of life, it is counterproductive to continue in unhealthy, non-enriching friendships that can make you feel bad about yourself and derail your progress. So let's examine the art of developing healthy friendships and enriching social circles.

MESSAGES MATTER

We've discussed the Eurocentric "thin ideal" promoted by the media and the impact it has on promoting body dissatisfaction

THE BLACK WOMAN'S BODY IMAGE DIET

in women, but there is another media-based message out there that is equally disturbing. It is so upsetting to watch the plethora of shows on television that are based on cattiness, backbiting, and disrespect among women in social circles. In fact, there's a whole franchise of reality TV shows that display the relationships of women this way. These women, under the guise of friendship, say the most horrible things to each other and about each other—and then they pack up and go on vacation together. It is utter foolishness. These examples are not representative of supportive social circles.

As is frequently demonstrated on reality TV, many women are extremely unkind to each other. Unfortunately, it appears that we are often equally unkind to ourselves. It has become so commonplace for women to verbally degrade their own bodies when they are alone, in the company of friends, or, worst of all, in front of young daughters and sons. Did you know that daughters of body-dissatisfied mothers likely become dissatisfied with their own bodies as well?[149] The careful selection of words could prevent our children from a future wrought with similar body image struggles.

What I am talking about here, for instance, is "fat talk," the term used to describe the self-degrading, thin-ideal-endorsing communication that goes on in female friendship groups.[150] Surely you have heard it, or perhaps even taken part in it. You know, statements like these:

"She is so thin, and I'm such a fat-ass."

"My gut is huge."

"I can't wear that blouse. My arms are too flabby."

"Ain't no way I'm gettin' in a bathing suit in public. You want me to get laughed outta the pool?"

MELINDA GORE

"I couldn't get my big toe in that dress if I tried."

"Look at the disgusting stretch marks on this big pot of mine."

"Yeah, I'm gonna drag my fat self to the gym again."

Sound familiar? Research shows that "fat talk," hearing it and particularly expressing it, promotes body dissatisfaction.[151] All the terrible things you say about yourself are nothing short of destructive. Many of us would never dare to say these things to the face of our worst enemy, these things we so casually say to ourselves and about ourselves to our friends. Although research suggests that African American females are less likely to engage in "fat talk" than White American females are, African American females may at times substitute other types of self-deprecating talk, particularly about their hair.[152] So take heed: Our messages can be as dangerous as weapons, so we must be careful about how we wield them. Clearly, this behavior is not the way to promote body positive living, and we can no longer participate in it or expose ourselves to it.

TIPS FOR CREATING EMPOWERING SOCIAL CIRCLES

To create an environment that promotes seeing yourself in a healthy, body positive way, I would like for you to exercise great care when building your social circles of support. Here are a few tips for improving your social circles, with the goal of promoting body positive thinking in yourself and others.

THE BLACK WOMAN'S BODY IMAGE DIET

Monitor your girl time. Start by becoming aware of the way you speak about your body to yourself. Then become aware of the way you speak about your body when you are around your girlfriends. Take inventory. How do your get-togethers with the girls sound? Are you encouraging each other? Are you sharing wonderful stories about family and other friends? Or is there a lot of negative body talk taking place? Maybe there is just too much talk about bodies in general—yours, theirs, or other bodies altogether. If you notice such talk, don't be afraid to confront it and change the subject or tone of the conversation. For instance, if a friend is worried that she'll look too fat in a dress she wants, public health expert Lenora Goodman recommends saying something like, "I think you should wear whatever makes you feel happy and confident."[153]

Become a positive body image ambassador. If you realize your time with the girls is filled with negative body talk, or "fat talk," share with them what you've learned. If you're comfortable doing so, share the vision you've created for yourself and what you are working toward. In other words, lead by example. After all, without an example, many women may not even recognize the negative body talk they engage in and how it may be impacting them or others.

As an ambassador for change, make it your first order of business to ban "fat talk" from your social circle. If, after a while, you notice that your friends still engage in "fat talk," then it's time for some tough talk—with yourself. Consider how important it is that you continue to move toward body positive living and feel great about yourself. Then evaluate the costs and benefits of holding on to those relationships. Remember my mother's wise words: "Mind the company you keep."

Show compassion for yourself and others. Not only is it important to be kind to yourself and watch the things you say about yourself around friends, but it is also important to extend this same compassion to others. Become mindful of how you treat other women you come into contact with. Do you tend to make judgments about how other women look or about what they should or should not be doing? If so, don't be so judgmental. Put yourself in their shoes for a minute. Maybe their self-critical little voice has been talking to them all day; don't you go adding to it. Just bite your tongue.

Seek new social circles. I understand that this one is tough because, as I mentioned earlier, women create strong bonds with other women. Furthermore, many of these relationships and the associated behaviors may have gone on for some time. Still, if your efforts to change the course of conversations within your social circles fall on deaf ears, I encourage you to surround yourself with different people—women who support your efforts to see yourself more positively. Seek relationships that are uplifting, encouraging, honest, and nurturing. Enter into relationships with women who are going where you want to go or have already arrived and can offer support as you work to get there too. This is crucial. Create supportive social circles that inspire you to do and become more.

THE BLACK WOMAN'S BODY IMAGE DIET

Give back. Because cultivating body positive living is not only about building a network of social support that feeds you, I encourage you to seek opportunities that support others as well. Helping others to overcome challenges of their own makes you feel good. Consider joining a women's group that is supportive, fun, and encouraging. Join a book club or start a book club. Join a fitness class, walking club, or cooking class. Better still, find an opportunity to volunteer. Did you know that volunteering can boost mood and well-being?[154] It also expands your social network. Giving back is great for building community, and it feels good too.

So far in this chapter, we have focused on friendships with women. However, these principles apply to relationships with men as well, whether they are boyfriends or "just" friends. Like your female friends, the men in your life can say things about you or other women that influence the way you think about your body. What happened to a friend of mine is a case in point. At the time, my friend was in her forties, a beautiful brown-skinned, brown-eyed woman of average height with chin-length relaxed hair. One night she was sitting with her date—a handsome, fit Black man—sipping cocktails at a happening spot in Harlem that was overflowing with gorgeous women of all shapes, shades, and sizes. At a table only a few feet away, the hostess seated a beautiful, tall, long-haired, light-skinned, light-eyed, model-esque Black woman—a Black exemplar of the Eurocentric standard of beauty. At the sight of this "ideal" woman, the date nudged my friend and whispered, "Now that's the kind of woman you marry." My friend's heart

MELINDA GORE

sank to her knees, but while fighting back tears, she smiled in agreement, then finished her meal, and kept a stiff upper lip the rest of the evening. Unfortunately, she continued to see this jerk for many more months, enduring his disrespect, until one day he just stopped coming around. Outrageous, huh? You're probably wondering, "How could he say such a thing to her? And how could she put up with it?" Consider, though, that often the men in our lives send us negative messages about our bodies without saying a word—when they turn to watch only European-looking beauties walk by or quintessential hip hop video vixens with large breasts, thick thighs and ample bottoms, or ogle them both in magazines, or on the screen.

I confess: I had to kiss a lot of frogs before I found a man who has made me feel like the most beautiful woman in the world every day since we said "I do." He says he is not blind to the so-called "ideal" body of the moment or the narrow standard of beauty that exists. "But," he tells me, "I value my obligation as a man to demonstrate my love, respect, and appreciation for you by not catcalling and hooting and hollering at women in or away from your presence. I take pride in knowing that the way I treat you, the way I see you and uphold you, is an acknowledgment to us both that you are 'fearfully and wonderfully made.'"

Now that's what I'm talking about! Keep your friends close and those who encourage you closer.

THE BLACK WOMAN'S BODY IMAGE DIET

BODY IMAGE BOOSTER: CREATING POSITIVE SOCIAL CIRCLES

Now that you know how integral enriching social circles are to your health and body positive living, engaging in social circles in a manner that supports your personal "healthstyle" is essential. Begin by reflecting on the times you have spent with others that really fueled you positively. Whether it was traveling with girlfriends, stepping with your sorors, shopping with your BFF, or playing cards with other couples, how did the interaction make you feel? What types of conversations were taking place? What was the setting like? Describe the atmosphere in the room. Give it some thought, and over the next few weeks make a list of ten new ideas for creating healthy, positive social circles. Over the next three months, map out a plan of action and incorporate those ideas into your social circle. After a bit of experimentation, add the ones that work well to your body positive living routine.

Step Nine

CREATE A HEALTHY HAVEN

Winston Churchill said, "We shape our dwellings and afterwards our dwellings shape us." I find these words to be wise, simple, and true. Have you ever walked into a room and immediately felt at home, like you could curl up in a comfy chair with a good book and stay there forever? I know I have. And now I look forward to that same feeling every time I come home.

At first glance, you may find it strange that I am including a chapter about your home and personal space in a book about body positive living. Just wait until you experience the bountiful benefits of a perfectly appointed space, and you will understand. Personally, this area of body positive living moves me like no other. It's unconventional, maybe. But when it comes to how you see and feel about yourself, there is a lot to be said about the place where you spend a great deal of your time. After all, your home is where you start and end your day. And if you are lucky, you get to spend a little time there in between. So the ninth step toward body positive living involves becoming more aware of how your surroundings impact the way you feel about yourself and your body.

MELINDA GORE

HOME IS YOUR RETREAT

When I consider the design of spaces, I am reminded of something I first heard Oprah say on her show many, many years ago. She said it again recently on oprahdaily.com because they are truly words to live by. She says: "your home should rise up and meet you when you walk through the door." I could not agree more. Your home should be a pleasant place, beautifully decorated to your liking. When you walk in the door, the space should be inviting and give you a sense of joy and pleasure. Your home is your retreat from the world. It is where you go to find peace, comfort, security, love, and joy. It should pleasantly stimulate all of your senses.

I have only recently completed formal study as an interior designer, but I have always been aware of the impact of my surroundings on the way I feel. I am intrigued by how motivated and productive I am when I am comforted by my space. I believe this is an untapped area of opportunity where you can really enhance your overall quality of life and the way you see and feel about your body.

If you are anything like me, you've probably watched your fair share of home improvement shows. A design team blows in and totally transforms a room or an entire house from a disorganized, jumbled, chaotic mess to something akin to a luxurious hotel suite. You've probably noticed the looks of amazement on the faces of the homeowners, the change in their demeanor that takes place right before your eyes. You see them go from hopeless to hopeful once their home has been modified. Sometimes the change is so overwhelming that the homeowners are brought to tears. It is as if the improvement to their surroundings has inspired them to believe that anything is possible.

Those television shows demonstrate how a beautifully designed space can promote feelings of happiness and gratitude. I invite you to explore how creating surroundings that you find pleasant and inviting and inspirational may improve how you see and feel about yourself. You don't have to undertake a major renovation to generate some of these positive feelings. Creating what I like to call a "healthy haven" doesn't require a whole new house of furniture or an expensive interior designer. Many of the ideas I will offer can be accomplished on your own. Just take it one project at a time. But, first, let's talk about the science behind all this.

THE SCIENCE OF DESIGN

There is a very cool, newly emerging field of design called *neuroarchitecture*. As the term indicates, it is the merging of neuroscience and architecture. It has to do with understanding the impact that design elements like light, space, and room layout have on physical and psychological well-being and how a person's surroundings influence brain processes involved with stress, memory, and emotion.[155] Neuroarchitecture is focused on everything from the purposeful design of homes and buildings to the impact of the design of entire cities on its residents. It is also making an impact in workplaces to improve productivity, in schools to facilitate learning, and in hospitals and other

MELINDA GORE

facilities where immediate changes to architecture may impact healing.[156] One study in particular found that hospital patients with windows in their rooms, allowing for views of nature, were discharged earlier than those surrounded by walls.[157]

A very important aspect of neuroarchitecture involves understanding how our physical space impacts hormones like serotonin and cortisol. In our discussion about feel-good foods in Step Six, we talked about neurotransmitters and the significant role they play in mood regulation. We learned how nutrients in the foods we eat impact these neurotransmitters, which then affect our mood. By consuming certain foods and eliminating others, we are better able to manage our mood, which in turn may be helpful in quieting that self-critical little inner voice.

I believe the same may be true concerning your surroundings. Imagine feeling overwhelmed by the daily demands of life. Now imagine walking into a home that is unorganized, chaotic, and in disarray. The resulting drop in mood may trigger poor food choices, poor exercise choices, decreased productivity, and possibly even your self-critical little voice—all of which could in turn sabotage your efforts toward body positive living. Now imagine walking into a comfortable, well-appointed, pleasurable environment at the end of a tough day. Notice the difference in how you feel? That boost may just improve your chances of engaging in the healthy behaviors that promote body positive living, including spending quiet time meditating, reading an inspirational book, or engaging in joyful movement.

THE BLACK WOMAN'S BODY IMAGE DIET

TIPS FOR CREATING YOUR HAVEN

So what does research tell us about the power of interior design to make us feel good or bad? The design of interior spaces may exert a positive or negative influence on five brain systems: sensation and perception, learning and memory, decision-making, emotion, and movement.[158] According to the research, there are a number of factors within your space that may impact your brain positively or negatively. Factors to consider are lighting, paint color, room layout, personal decor, use of natural and smooth materials, mirrors, privacy, organization, and scents and sounds. While all of these features can affect how you feel about your body by lifting or depressing your spirits, some can directly affect the way you see yourself. Let us take a closer look at each one.

> **Lighting.** Nothing can evoke a mood or set the tone of a space better than lighting. There are multiple sources of light, including natural sunlight, bright light for tasks, and candles and lights with dimmers to create the perfect ambience. As best you can, utilize different forms of light throughout your home to promote improved mood. It is a small change that may have a large impact. Open your blinds and curtains to let in that highly beneficial natural light. Exposure to daylight increases productivity and comfort and helps to regulate the body's circadian rhythms (the biological clock that helps the body adapt to the cycle of day and night). Light is even used to treat some forms of depression because it promotes the release of the mood-boosting hormone serotonin.[159]

MELINDA GORE

However, lighting affects not only your mood but also the image of yourself that you see in the mirror, on Zoom, or in photos. Any professional photographer will tell you that lighting affects how you look, regardless of your skin color. If you're in harsh, direct sunlight, the sun will cast shadows into the creases of your face and exaggerate the lumps and bumps in your body. In contrast, the diffused light on a cloudy day will soften your face, while the golden light from a setting sun will illuminate your hair with a warm glow.[160] Indoor light is trickier. Because artificial light has a noticeable tint, it can make your teeth and skin and the whites of your eyes look sickly. Overhead lighting is worse since it can cast shadows on your face that make your face look longer or shorter, your nose look wider or narrower, and your eyes look like little black holes.[161] Of all the artificial lights we use in our homes, fluorescent light is probably the least flattering. It highlights wrinkles, smile lines, crow's feet, blemishes, and bags under your eyes; it makes you look pale or unhealthy; and it even changes the color of your makeup.[162] On top of that, fluorescent light can increase stress, eye strain, and headaches too.[163] So if you have fluorescent lights in your home, replace them with soft white or daylight bulbs. If you're videoconferencing during the daytime, face a window but adjust the blinds if necessary to avoid direct rays; then, at night, illuminate your face in the warm glow of a lamp. And if you're taking selfies or posing for photos, try to situate yourself in soft, diffused light, whether you're indoors or outdoors.

THE BLACK WOMAN'S BODY IMAGE DIET

The power of paint. Paint color is powerful as well, and it can have a major impact on mood. If you have ever strolled through the paint department at any home improvement store, you know the color choices are practically endless. While the actual science behind the effect of color on mental state is somewhat anecdotal, it does not negate the impact color may have on you. Whether it is the actual color itself or the memories triggered by particular colors, this is an area worth exploring. It offers an excellent opportunity for some personal, single-subject research to become aware of how color affects you.

Try adding colors to your space that promote more of the outcomes you would like to see. For example, pink is thought to be calming and relaxing. Many police stations around the country have pink drunk tanks (the areas where they hold intoxicated inmates) for this very reason.[164] Red is thought to increase memory and retention of information. It can increase heart rate, so it may be more suitable for a home office or kitchen. Blue, which belongs to the family of "cool" colors, is believed to promote creativity, harmony, and feelings of relaxation. It makes a wonderful choice for bathrooms and bedrooms.

I think we can all agree that yellow promotes optimism and is an overall very cheerful color. Places within your home where you want to encourage conversation and interaction may be suitable for a beautiful yellow hue, like a living room or kitchen. Green often symbolizes good health and rejuvenation, and orange is great for promoting energy and friendliness. If you really want to elevate your space for optimal benefits, consider purple. Purple has always been associated with royalty, but it is also believed to promote wisdom and spirituality.[165] While you may not paint an entire room any of these colors, they do make for great accents that could brighten your space as well as your mood. Use the color on a wall, a floor, a ceiling, or even select pieces of furniture. You can even incorporate accent colors into rooms via pillows, rugs, or throws.

Room layout. Feng shui is a widely accepted practice built on the principles of proper placement of items in a room in an effort to harmonize individuals with their surrounding environment. It originated in China thousands of years ago. Many of today's interior design practices are also inspired by the balance that room layout and furniture placement provide. The flow of a room leads to feelings of relaxation, ease, and comfort. The kitchen is often referred to as the heart of the home. Research shows that an open kitchen floor plan that allows you to face your family or guests while preparing food actually causes the brain to release serotonin and oxytocin, hormones associated with relaxation, enjoyment, and bonding.[166] Kitchens that face away from your family or guests do just the opposite, promoting the release of stress- and anxiety-related hormones like cortisol and adrenaline.[167] Of course, I am not suggesting that you tear down walls and completely remodel your kitchen space if your current layout does not allow you to face your family. But this knowledge does give you insight into what is taking place and how you may alter meal preparation

THE BLACK WOMAN'S BODY IMAGE DIET

to include your family, to keep your stress levels low and spirits high, and to facilitate that "kitchen table talk" that has played such a vital role in Black families throughout our history.

Consider as well the layout of your other rooms and the arrangement of your furniture. Try placing your sofa in a way that allows you to look out a window to enjoy a beautiful view. On the other hand, placing furniture around a fireplace may elicit feelings of warmth and comfort.

Yet another feature in your space that can evoke your brain's response is ceiling height. Some people believe that if you thrive on creativity, tall ceilings may be best to encourage this type of thinking since they activate the right side of the brain, which is responsible for abstract and creative thinking. Research suggests that there may be something to this belief. In an experiment conducted at the University of Minnesota, people were assigned tasks that favored either abstract or detail-oriented thinking. Researchers found that people focused more on specific details when the ceiling height was eight feet high and focused more on the abstract when the ceiling was ten feet high.[168] These are all things to consider when designing and decorating your space.

Personal decor. Another way to elicit feelings of comfort in your home is to decorate with personal possessions that you hold dear. There is no better place to showcase your personal style than within your home. Frame photos of memorable times with family and friends and mount them on walls and throughout your space. If you've taken a trip that holds special memories, prominently display some of the souvenirs you brought back, whether they're shells from the Caribbean, wooden carvings from Africa, or Navajo vases from the Southwest. Search online and within specialty shops for items that represent who you are and cause you to feel at peace. The display of personal items in your home allows you to express your individuality and keeps you feeling grounded and comfortable.

Natural and smooth materials. Using natural materials within your space, like granite, marble, wood, greenery, and water rather than man-made materials are wonderful ways to promote positive feelings in your home. Greenery especially. According to the concept of biophilia, humans have an instinctive resonance with other living things, including plants. The body's response to these items may have a major impact on your mood and health. Plants and even pictures of landscapes can reduce stress and promote increased concentration.[169] Bringing in fresh flowers or getting in touch with your green thumb by decorating with potted plants can be beneficial as well. As a bonus, having greenery in your immediate environment improves air quality—this is a win-win if you ask me. Additionally, aim to decorate with end tables, coffee tables, and sofas that have smooth, rounded surfaces. Sharp edges trigger the brain to be on the lookout for danger, which makes it hard to relax.[170] Smooth, rounded surfaces and materials elicit the opposite effect.

THE BLACK WOMAN'S BODY IMAGE DIET

Mirrors. It is my opinion that mirrors play an important role in our positive body image journey and should not be avoided. They present excellent opportunities to compliment yourself or find something about your body you truly appreciate. They also serve as great motivational tools. The bathroom mirror is where I give myself some of my best and most needed morning pep talks before heading out for the day. However, I understand that mirrors may not hold the same value for everyone, and that's okay. It's important to include in your space those things that support your body image.

Did you know, though, that mirrors can be used to help individuals who have eating disorders see themselves more positively? Called "mirror exposure therapy," this treatment offers us a lot to learn because the most promising improvements in body satisfaction are experienced when the person looking into the mirror is kind, gentle, and appreciative of the reflection she sees. Even if she doesn't believe it at first, with continued practice she can experience incremental changes toward greater body satisfaction.[171]

Privacy. If you live with others, it is important to carve out a little space of your very own. Loud noise, constant distractions, and an overall lack of adequate privacy can leave you feeling stressed. Perhaps you can convert a small closet or unused room into your personal sanctuary. Having a space of your own allows you to experience peace and calm in an otherwise chaotic environment. Outfit it with a collection of the things you love that are mood elevating and enjoyable too.

Bring in pillows, a throw, and a lamp so it can serve as a peaceful space for prayer or meditation. You may appreciate such a spot even if you live alone.

Organization. "A place for everything and everything in its place" are words to live by. Keeping items in your home tidy and in good working order helps to keep your mind clear. Aim to keep your desk free and clear of clutter. Doing so lends to increased productivity.[172] Designate a space for keys, toys, and mail as well. This is extremely beneficial in cutting down the stress that can arise when you need things in a hurry. It is not necessary to have a perfectly clean space in order to experience the benefits of organization. Rather, imagine if you will, finding a happy place somewhere between clutter and perfection.

Scents and sounds. Don't overlook the importance of bringing in beautiful scents and calming sounds. Each impacts our mood. Essential oils have a multitude of healthful benefits as do organic, clean-burning candles. A girlfriend shared with me once that each time she goes on a special vacation, she purchases a new fragrance or scent during her travels. When she is back home and needs to be reminded of her relaxing time, she simply fills the room with the scent. Instantly, she's able to return to that place. You can easily accomplish this with essential oils, scented candles, or perfume. Conduct a little research to determine which scents best suit your needs. The same goes for sounds. Technology has given us plenty of ways to incorporate soothing sounds into our environments, from sound machines to built-in architectural fountains and streams.

Regardless of which ideas you choose to incorporate into your interior space, in keeping with *The Black Woman's Body Image Diet*, it is important to personalize this step. Again, creating a space that lifts your mood does not need to be overwhelming or overly expensive. Simply take it one room at a time, one project at a time, or even one item at a time. We spoke earlier about the importance of keeping boredom at bay with your joyful movement routine. The same applies to your home. Little changes can really help to combat feelings of stagnation. Changes as small as rearranging the living room furniture or replacing a few lights may do the trick. Notice how your mood and your self-perception shift when you devote some TLC to your surroundings.

BODY IMAGE BOOSTER: DESIGN YOUR HEALTHY HAVEN

1. Create a vision for your dream space. Gather a few of your favorite home decor catalogs or magazines and clip photos of the items you would like to include in your healthy haven. Create your own little designer's portfolio, complete with floor plans, furniture placement, paints, and fabrics. Refer to it often. This will probably be an ongoing process as your tastes and needs tend to change, but continue to add to it anyway. Once your vision is clear, select a project, get an accurate quote, and pinpoint a date on your calendar to get started.

MELINDA GORE

2. Visit the home improvement store near you, gather paint swatches, and determine which colors you are drawn to. Take note of the responses they trigger in your mood and overall feelings. Gather fabric swatches of textures you'd like to include in your space. Come up with plans—whether with paint, fabric, or otherwise—to include these items in your surroundings right away.

Step Ten

PAMPER YOURSELF TO ENHANCE YOUR HEALTH *AND* BEAUTY

I realize that this step toward body-positive living may be difficult for many to understand. In a program that encourages you to reject society's impossible beauty standards, it may seem inappropriate that I am including a conversation about healthy skin and hair, flattering clothing and accessories, and beautiful makeup and nails. I understand your concern, but please allow me to explain.

As I mentioned at the start of this book, I worked as a makeup artist for many years. I have a true appreciation for makeup artistry, and I have seen firsthand the way many women come to life once they discover the little things about makeup that make a pretty big difference in the way they see themselves: simple things like finding the perfect shade of lipstick, curling lashes for the first time, or learning the tricks to cover dark under-eye circles in a way that makes them appear rested and refreshed.

MELINDA GORE

It is powerful to watch little things like these almost *instantly* improve the way so many women see and feel about themselves. Haven't you had similar feelings after an appointment with your hair stylist? When your hair is freshly cut, colored, and/or styled, doesn't it lift your mood and cause you to feel better about your appearance?

The act of setting aside time, on an otherwise busy day, to care for yourself has its benefits. While I do not believe or support the idea that your value, worth, or beauty is determined by outward appearance, I do believe that taking care of your skin, hair, clothing, and personal grooming is an important part of self-care, which is the tenth step toward body positive living. Together, we will navigate the thin line between health and beauty.

A THIN LINE

There is a very thin line between health and beauty. Many self-care practices performed to enhance beauty are beneficial to your health. Likewise, many self-care practices that promote health have beauty benefits as well. Benefits like reduced stress, improved mood, positive outlook, and increased quality of life are just as likely to be the outcome of health-driven self-care practices as beauty-driven self-care practices.

WellCoaches describes self-care as a way of living that incorporates the behaviors that enable one to maintain personal health and balance, replenish energy and motivation, and grow as a person.[173] With such an inclusive definition as this, you can imagine that a variety of behaviors fall under the umbrella of

THE BLACK WOMAN'S BODY IMAGE DIET

self-care. No doubt about it, eating feel-good foods and exercising for enjoyment are forms of self-care, and both contribute to your health in a multitude of ways. Taking a break from your cellphone to go for a nice long walk in nature constitutes self-care. Scheduling a bit of time in your day to unplug and laugh a little constitutes self-care. Seeing your physician for regular check-ups and your dentist for routine cleanings is self-care. Getting regular mammograms and conducting monthly breast self-examinations is self-care, as is taking your medications as prescribed. I also believe that tending to your appearance—which contributes to your health in a multitude of ways—is a form of self-care as well. If you think about it, everything we have discussed so far is self-care: eating feel-good foods, engaging in joyful movement, practicing positive self-talk, practicing prayer and meditation, spending time with encouraging friends, purposefully designing our homes, and now taking steps to enhance our appearance. To say it plainly, body positive living *is* self-care.

But won't caring for your appearance focus too much of your attention on your looks? *The Black Woman's Body Image Diet* embraces the idea that we are more than our physical body, our dress size, or our scale weight. Yes, this is still our belief; nothing has changed. As you learned from our earlier discussion, body positive living requires creating and modeling your own idea of beauty despite a barrage of messages that seek to undermine it. However, a new definition of beauty need not exclude your desire to put your best foot forward and take special care of your appearance. I do not believe that women must neglect their hair, go without makeup, ignore their skin, or shun flattering clothing in order to take a stand against the media's limited beauty ideal. What good does that do? Wearing a hairstyle that you like, taking time to care for and protect your skin, and finding makeup and clothing that are flattering—all have a place in self-care and body positive living. When you make the effort to look good, you feel good, you feel proud, and, as a result, you feel more confident about your body.

I realize it is often difficult for us, as women, to figure out how to present ourselves to the world. That's why society's narrow standard of beauty has had such an enormous impact on so many American women, including Black women. If you don't believe me, consider this: Women were responsible for 85 percent of the spending on beauty products in this country in 2017.[174] According to the Nielsen report, in 2017, Black consumers accounted for nearly 90 percent of the spending on ethnic hair and beauty aids.[175]

I understand well the argument that the choices women make about aesthetic beauty are not actually choices at all but rather are forced upon women, who in turn feel pressured by society to make certain decisions. In spite of all that, ultimately, the choices are yours to make, not anyone else's. So, as always, I encourage you to adopt only the steps that you find suitable for your personal journey toward body positive living. If enhancing your appearance in these areas of self-care appeals to you, I encourage you to find a way to make them personal and incorporate them into your life. Now let's take a closer look.

SELF-CARE MAINTENANCE

I like to think of health-and-beauty self-care as the frosting on the cake. When other aspects of your life are in order and you have a plan in place to improve the areas that need to be improved, taking the time to enhance your beauty regimen is just another great way to elevate the way you see and feel about your body. It is perfectly okay to have a little fun and spruce things up by tending to your appearance. It's all about finding new ways to feel good about yourself—not for anyone else, but just for you.

It really is the little things that make the biggest difference. I am reminded of a dear friend of mine. She never went to the gym without a perfectly coordinated workout ensemble. Her T-shirt, shorts, sneakers, and hair accessories always matched. The wonderful part was that she didn't do it because she was concerned about the opinions of others. She did it because it made her feel good about herself and added the extra boost she needed to get through her workouts. She provides the perfect example of incorporating the little things that cause you to feel good about yourself and personalizing the journey toward body positive living.

Exploring fun new ways to upgrade your daily routine fits right in with this concept, which I like to refer to as "self-care maintenance." It includes the areas of facial care, body care, makeup, hair, nails, clothing, and accessories. Together with all the other areas of body positive living you are working on, taking the time to manage your self-care maintenance routine is equally important in improving the way you see and feel about your body. Let's jump right in.

MELINDA GORE

Facial care. Taking care of and protecting your skin will go a long way toward helping you feel good about the way you see yourself. Your skin is the largest organ of the body, and the first thing people see when they come in contact with you, especially your face. Interestingly enough, a clear, glowing complexion is often the result of many of the other health-promoting activities this book has encouraged you to adopt as a part of body positive living. Drinking lots of water, eating plenty of healthy, feel-good foods, and engaging in joyful movement that makes you sweat all lead to beautiful skin. While healthy food and exercise will help you take care of your skin from the inside, finding good skincare products will allow you to do the same for the outside. Let's face it, we tend to have a little more pep in our step on those clear-skin days. Rarely does anyone have perfectly even skin all the time, but it's important to implement a skincare routine which includes quality products that are appropriate for your skin type. A suitable skin care routine for your face should include makeup remover, cleanser, an exfoliant, toner, eye cream, and a moisturizer with sunscreen.

Now, sisters, I know what some of you are thinking right now: "*I* don't need sunscreen." Indeed you do! Although Black people are less likely to suffer from sunburn, our "magic melanin" will not protect us from the dangerous UV rays that cause melanoma and other types of skin cancer. Even dark skin has a sun protection factor (SPF)

THE BLACK WOMAN'S BODY IMAGE DIET

of only 13, when an SPF of 30 is the minimum dermatologists recommend. In addition, Black people are more likely to suffer from lupus and high blood pressure, conditions that increase skin sensitivity to the sun's harmful UV rays.

Historically, there has been a dearth of research and medical training focused on Black people's skin, but here's what we do know: Black people are 1½ times more likely to die from melanoma than White people because Blacks are 4 times more likely to be diagnosed later when the cancer has reached an advanced stage. So, sisters, wear sunscreen. Sure, mineral-based sunscreen can leave an ugly white film on your face, even if you're light-skinned. But after decades of marketing and manufacturing geared toward only White people, the landscape of the sunscreen industry is finally showing signs of change. Thanks to a forward-thinking Black female entrepreneur who recognized the need to address the specific sun protection concerns of Black people, who entered the market with her appropriately named Black Girl Sunscreen that protects your melanin, smells and feels amazing and won't leave an ashy residue on your skin.[176] Also, although you may have grown up hearing, "Black don't crack," keep in mind that your melanin may not protect your skin from UVA rays, the UV rays that can lead to premature skin aging, such as wrinkles, age spots, and sagging. That means applying a moisturizer with at least 30 SPF every day can protect your looks as well as your health.

MELINDA GORE

I would be remiss if I ended this discussion of facial care without mentioning skin bleaching, the practice of using creams, soaps, pills, or injections to lighten the skin. You may wonder why I feel I must bring up the topic. Rooted in the white supremacy of colonialism and slavery—and the colorism it produced among people of color—skin bleaching is widely condemned in the U.S. nowadays. Perhaps you assume, then, that lightening dark skin is a thing of the past in the U.S., that it is prevalent today only in parts of Africa and Asia. While it is true that the practice is less common today among African Americans, it persists among some African and Afro-Caribbean immigrants in the U.S. Moreover, as Yaba Blay, a leading scholar on colorism recently observed, "If you open up a U.S. magazine where the audience is primarily Black women, you're going to see ads of products that are made to 'even out skin tones.' If you go to a beauty supply store right now, there are entire aisles dedicated to skin-bleaching products that I can find in Ghana *and in Brooklyn*. The fact that the shelves remain stocked lets us know that the product is as active as it is there."[177] In fact, in the U.S. in 2020, women of color reportedly purchased more than two billion dollars' worth of skin-lightening products.[178] Clearly, skin bleaching persists because colorism persists—as well as the drive for corporations to make a profit off it.

So if you have been using a product to "even out" your skin tone, check the label. Do the ingredients include mercury, hydroquinone, or corticosteroids? If so,

THE BLACK WOMAN'S BODY IMAGE DIET

beware. These substances have been associated with health problems ranging from dermatitis to kidney damage. Now ask yourself whether you have been trying to "even out" your complexion or trying to look lighter. Be honest with yourself. If it's the former, good news: we're going to discuss foundations that can give Black women that even tone. But if it's the latter, hopefully, having read Part I of this book, you have created a new definition of beauty that celebrates your Blackness and have armed yourself with new strategies to protect yourself from messages that promote Whiteness.

Body care. Beautiful skin doesn't stop at your face. For soft, hydrated, evenly toned, beautiful skin all over, the options are unlimited. As the seasons change, our skin does too. Find a body wash or shower gel appropriate for each season; for instance, a body wash with extra moisturizers for dry winter skin or one with extra cleansers for sweaty summer skin. Pair it with a loofah or exfoliating gloves when you need to, and you will be amazed by how beautiful and soft your skin can be. Find an all-natural body moisturizer, body oil, or body butter, and apply it daily from head to toe. Moisturizing daily is especially important if your knees and elbows look ashy. Ashy skin is just dry skin, but it's more noticeable the darker you are. To treat ashy skin, apply creams, oils, ointments or quality lotions that lock in moisture. Your skin will thank you! There are some really great brands out there, including Black-owned brand Urban Hydration, who

MELINDA GORE

truly understand the unique needs of our skin.[179] Keep experimenting until you find the ones you like.

Another wonderful thing you can do for your skin is body brushing. Not only does it slough away dead skin cells, but it serves as a mode of detoxification as well.[180] Just get yourself a large, soft bristle brush. Brush your skin starting at your feet, working all the way up to your neck. Be sure to stroke your skin with soft, gentle brushes toward your heart. I find the best time for body brushing is first thing in the morning just before showering.

Makeup. Now, I don't know about you, but I am a bit of a makeup junkie. I simply cannot get enough. I am constantly on the lookout for the next new thing. However, if you're not a makeup wearer, by no means am I trying to convince you that you should be. I am merely suggesting that you consider giving it a try. As I mentioned earlier, I have witnessed firsthand how women who never wore makeup or who wore makeup that was ill-suited for them changed before my eyes when they found the right makeup and received some guidance in applying it skillfully and tastefully.

There are many good brands of cosmetics for Black women. Gone are the days when we had to struggle with mismatched foundation and eye or lip colors that clashed with our skin colors. Nowadays there are Black female-owned brands with shades and formulations

THE BLACK WOMAN'S BODY IMAGE DIET

made just for us, brands such as Mented Cosmetics, The Lip Bar, Marjani Beauty, Prime Beauty Cosmetics, and, of course, Rihanna's multimillion-dollar brand, Fenty Beauty.[181] And I am so pleased to announce that Fashion Fair Cosmetics is back! Under the leadership of two amazing Black female entrepreneurs, Desiree Rogers and Cheryl Mayberry McKissack, this brand began as an homage to the glamour, fashion and beauty of Black women. Here we are 49 years later and the products are vegan and better than ever, offering a diverse spectrum of ethnic skin tones.[182] In addition to these great brands, there are cosmetic lines specially designed for mature women since as we age, our skin changes: fine lines appear, eyebrows thin, skin sags below the eyes. Take, for instance, L'Oreal's Age Perfect line, which includes serum concealers, magnifying eyebrow pencils, firming foundation, and hydrating lipstick for the 50+ woman.

However, makeup is not about changing who you are or hiding who you are or trying to become someone else. If you spend any amount of time on social media, you're probably familiar with the makeup contouring tutorials that truly transform faces. The techniques are amazing and fun to watch, but I can't help but notice that the goals of contouring all seem to be the same, thinner noses and faces, higher cheekbones and high-lighters to lighten skin tones, all of which are consis-tent with today's narrow beauty standards. The artistry is gorgeous, and great for photography, but not at all

MELINDA GORE

necessary for you to look and feel beautiful. Makeup founder Bobbi Brown says, "Makeup is a way to help women look and feel like themselves, only prettier and more confident."[183] I totally agree. If you are new to makeup, stop by a good department store or beauty retailer for guidance. After a solid skincare routine, the most important place to begin is with a beautiful, natural-looking foundation to even your skin tone. Here's a tip: opt for a tinted moisturizer rather than a heavy foundation for a natural look and to keep your complexion even and fresh looking.

Hair. Our hair, a lot like our skin, is one of the first things we present to the world. Having great-looking hair is another thing that can help you feel fantastic about yourself. Unfortunately, as I noted earlier, having "Black-looking" hair makes many Black women feel bad about themselves. Because typical Black hair differs so much from the Eurocentric ideal of long, straight, blonde hair, Black women in this country have a long history of exploring creative new ways of making their hair look longer, straighter, or lighter. For generations, unless they were born with so-called "good hair" (i.e., straight, wavy, or loosely curled hair), many Black women invested inordinate amounts of time and/or money trying to transform their hair. In this era when natural Black hairstyles have become increasingly popular, some Black women still opt to lengthen their hair by adding extensions or weaves. Some straighten their hair with hot combs and

THE BLACK WOMAN'S BODY IMAGE DIET

chemical relaxers. And some lighten their hair with dyes. Others opt for the ease of wearing wigs. Extensions, weaves and wigs also serve as great protective styles as well. So many options!

Now don't get me wrong. I'm not saying that making these hair choices is bad. Personally, I am so thankful for beautifully crafted wigs and weaves. So if long or straight or blonde hair truly makes you feel your best, then be my guest. Just make sure you examine your motives: Why do you believe you look prettier this way? Are you equating prettiness with Whiteness because you grew up bombarded by negative messages about "nappy" or "kinky" Black hair and positive messages about long, silky White hair? Or are you worried about what other people would think if you sported a natural hairstyle? Or is it something else altogether? Is it pressure to conform to society's definition of "professional?" According to a new report, hair discrimination persists, especially in the workplace. And it's not just discrimination by Whites.[184] I'll never forget what happened when I told the Black male hair stylist I had been seeing for years that I wanted to stop relaxing my hair. He simply said, "You're a beautiful woman, and you deserve a good man. Trust me, you do not want the type of man that natural hair is going to attract."

Whatever your motivation may be, if you are relaxing or dyeing your hair, be mindful of the health risks. A recent study found that Black women who used lye-based hair

MELINDA GORE

relaxers at least 7 times a year for 15 years or more were 30 percent more likely to develop breast cancer than less-frequent users. As for hair dye, you would think that there would be no such health disparity since both Black and White women color their hair, whether they are trying to lighten it or cover the gray. But, apparently, there is. Another recent study found that Black women were more likely to develop breast cancer from using permanent hair dye: For Black women, the risk was an astonishing 45 percent compared with a 7 percent risk for White female users.[185] So far, the American Cancer Society says the body of research on cancer risks from permanent hair dye is inconclusive.[186] But if this recent finding is reliable, it does not bode well for Black women since we are more likely to develop breast cancer before age 40, more likely to suffer from an aggressive form of breast cancer, and 40 percent more likely to die from it.[187] In other words, our hair dissatisfaction—and the institutions that foster it—may be killing us.

So what should you do with your hair? Weigh the risks and benefits. Then, if you decide to continue using a relaxer or dye, try relaxers without lye and semi-permanent or temporary dyes, including glosses, glazes, and henna. In general, try to keep your hair as healthy as possible. As is the case with your skin, exercise and a healthy diet both contribute to a beautiful, healthy head of hair. For Black hair, so do moisturizers and oil: the tighter the curl or coil, the more moisturizers and oil are needed.[188] Keep

THE BLACK WOMAN'S BODY IMAGE DIET

your hair healthy with good maintenance, but also consider exploring safe ways to enhance your hair's appearance. You've seen those makeover shows; a little expert styling can change your life. Try a bold, new temporary color, a sassy new cut, or maybe extensions that aren't permanent. Or experiment with a natural style. Back in the day, "going natural" meant wearing an Afro, but today there are so many other options: cornrows, braids, twists, and Bantu knots, to name a few. They can be a lot of fun when you just want to change things up.

If you don't already have a great stylist who knows what they are doing, I urge you to find one. Ask for a referral from a friend whose hair you like or go online and do some research. I am a firm believer that every woman should have her "beauty trinity" in place and on speed dial at all times: a good hairstylist, makeup artist, and esthetician.

Nails. I'm all for getting regular manicures and pedicures. There's something about picking a nail color that makes you feel good and slipping on your cutest peep toe pumps and having a little fun being you. So go ahead—show off your flashy nail colors and exquisite nail designs on those two-inch talons! Your ability to express yourself is a powerful component of body positive living. However, it is also important to be mindful of the impact of your expression on your health. We are constantly bombarded with potentially harmful toxins through air pollution, household cleaners, pesticides, preservatives, food additives, heavy metals, and plastics used in every-day life. We have to be vigilant to keep toxins out when and wherever possible—especially when it comes to beauty products.

Our skin is permeable, including our nails. Every layer of product that we apply has the potential to enter our bloodstream. And even though a number of products are available on the market and not considered danger-ous, no one is really talking about what happens when we use all those products together. Did you know that most American women apply up to 168 different chemi-cals from lotions, fragrances, makeups, and soaps on a daily basis? This combination contributes to toxic load, and over time our organs may struggle to properly filter out these toxins and impurities. We've already spoken a bit about the dangers of relaxers and hair dyes, but nail polish is included as well. The key is limiting the use of so many products and, whenever possible, choosing all-natural options that are free of ingredients known to have adverse effects on your body.[189] I encourage you to check the EWG Skin Deep cosmetics database to de-termine whether any of the ingredients in your beauty products are toxic.[190]

Clothing. We've talked about how your choices and hab-its regarding your health determine your personal "health-style," but your personal style drives your preferences, and it affects nearly everything you do. When it comes to developing your personal wardrobe style, I encourage you to find your own and allow it to evolve over time. Get a real sense of the image you'd like to portray to the world. Find the style of clothing, fabrics, and colors that suit you best. Identify a style muse, someone whose style you admire, and allow them to inspire your own. Or hire a personal stylist to help you home in on your best features and to locate clothing that fits well and plays up those positive features, perhaps the color of your eyes or skin. Always begin with properly fitting undergarments. Appropriately sized bras, panties and shapewear can change your life. I can't overemphasize the importance of good fit for your undergarments as well as your other clothing. By taking the time to find the appropriate fit, you can use clothes to build body confidence. Evidence shows that women with overall body dissatisfaction are generally less satisfied with the fit of their clothes.[191] No matter what your size is, a balanced top and bottom with a defined waist is helpful. Remember, though, dressing well is not about looking like someone else but about cultivating a style that suits you. So if you like to step out dressed in purple from head to toe or you like to sashay around town in a traditional African gown, you go, girl! Do your thing!

Accessories. The accessories we wear with our clothing can be another standout part of our wardrobe. Accessories allow us to share our stories, and often they speak louder than words. As a matter of fact, accessories are a form of non-verbal communication giving the world a glimpse into who we are, plus so much more. Accessories have a special way of boosting our confidence and making us feel beautiful.

Whether it's a scarf worn around your neck or intricately wrapped around your curly tresses, each provides another avenue to highlight your personality. The same goes for shoes, sunglasses, handbags, and hats. Especially shoes and hats. For many women, shoes are the one thing they can always depend on for that immediate confidence boost. Weight fluctuations may rule out many things in your closet on a given day, but you can always count on a cute pair of pumps to make you feel like everything is right with world. As for hats, whether they are Sunday hats, leather caps, or African head wraps, they have given generations of Black women extra spark or sass. In our culture we refer to our hats as well as our hairdos as "crowns," and the style we choose is one of the many ways we express ourselves. And what a statement a hat can make! Think of the 82-year-old Black woman who wore a different hat every Sunday for over 50 weeks when her church went online during the pandemic. Why? Because it made her feel good. Do you have a hat, cap, or head wrap that makes you feel like a million dollars?

But let's not forget my personal favorite: jewelry. Whether it's an heirloom or a lucky flea-market find, whether it's

THE BLACK WOMAN'S BODY IMAGE DIET

a little bit of "bling" or a hip hop "jewelry drip," jewelry has the unquestionable ability to bring out a woman's best. I'm a firm believer that every woman should have a signature piece of jewelry—a single item that uniquely represents who you are. For many mothers, it's a piece that showcases every child's birthstone. For others, it's the right-hand ring that says, "Yes, my left hand shows that I am married, but my right hand shows that I am still uniquely me." I have always worn a delicate sterling silver necklace with the letter "M" written in script. It's not the most expensive piece, but it has been there resting against my collarbone for what feels like forever. If you don't already have one, you may be surprised what you'll learn about yourself in finding that one special something that speaks to/for you.

There are a million other ways to incorporate self-care into your daily routine. I understand that none of us will die without a mani/pedi or a good bikini wax. That is not what we are talking about here. We are just talking about the little ways that allow us to care for ourselves and contribute to feeling great. For instance, schedule a full body massage. This is such a wonderful way to wind down and relax. Not to mention, massage has therapeutic benefits of its own. If you're not into full body massage, start with a soothing scalp or foot massage. Other fun self-care ideas include brow waxes, lip waxes, ear candling, aromatherapy, warm baths, daytime naps, restorative sleep, orchestrating your perfect wind-down ritual in the evenings, keeping a gratitude journal, and spa days.

MELINDA GORE

ONE MORE THOUGHT

I would like to leave you with one more thought before we move on to the Conclusion. Self-care is important, but it's not just those deeply pampering things that constitute self-care. It really is everything that contributes to the proper care of your body. It is important to watch the foods you eat and get enough exercise, but it is super important to stay on top of all aspects of your health as well. I guarantee that whatever sort of self-care you indulge in, you'll thank yourself for making time to take care of *you*.

BODY IMAGE BOOSTER: CREATE A SELF-CARE PLAN

Create your own self-care plan this week. As you've just learned, there are a multitude of options for health and beauty self-care practices. A great place to start is determining what is important to you. What do you value most about self-care? Is it the health benefits? The beauty benefits? Both? Is it making yourself a priority? Get out your Body Positive Living journal and take a moment to brainstorm all the ways you can imagine that you would like to implement self-care practices based on the things that are important to you. Remember, this is brainstorming. There are no limitations and no judgments. Once you have a nice long list, narrow it down to the things you are most interested in exploring. Once your brainstorming is narrowed down,

THE BLACK WOMAN'S BODY IMAGE DIET

identify three self-care practices that you would like to experience within the next three months. That's one per month over the next three months, which gives you plenty of time to experiment. Undoubtedly, you will find a few things you love and others you do not. Once you settle on a few favorites, add them to your body positive living routine.

Conclusion

SPREAD THE WORD, CHANGE THE WORLD

It is bittersweet that we live in a society that is so connected socially. Today, you have the ability to reach out to just about anyone around the globe to spread messages of hope and positivity from your laptop or cellphone with just a few taps of your finger. But I say bittersweet because just as easily and quickly as positivity can be spread, so can hate and negativity.

The media has portrayed the same narrow definition of beauty for years and will likely continue for years to come if we don't take a stand. So now is your chance. I encourage you to make it a priority to share messages of hope and positivity. You are now armed with a game plan for body positive living propelled by a new definition of beauty. By all means, post it and tweet it. Scream it from the rooftops. Let's sign petitions and write letters to those responsible for the images we see. Let's contact our state representatives and show support for bills like The Crown Act. The Crown Act, which stands for Creating

MELINDA GORE

a Respectful and Open World for Natural Hair, is a law that prohibits race-based hair discrimination.[192] Allow your voice to be heard. Let's give our business to publications and organizations that promote an inclusive message of beauty. Let's spread the word and change the world. Spread the word that beauty comes in all shapes, shades, and sizes and change the world as we know it into a place where everyone is encouraged to celebrate their beauty even if it is different from the so-called "ideal."

As I mentioned earlier, younger and younger girls are now dealing with body image issues all the time. It is problematic that, in our culture, little girls as young as three would worry about weight and physical appearance.[193] It is up to us as moms, stepmoms, sisters, aunts, and friends to start the conversation among ourselves first and then share this body positive message early on with every young girl so that she has a fair chance to enjoy all life has to offer. It's important to start early. Research suggests that instilling confidence and building a positive body image in children at an early age has a bearing on how they deal with challenges in later years.[194] Especially our little Black girls. Little Black girls everywhere need and deserve to hear that they are smart and pretty. I personally make it a point to smile and compliment them at every encounter. Mostly because it warms my heart to see them light up from the inside, but also because I know what it meant to me as little Black girl to be acknowledged in that way. Trust me, they may not have words to describe it, but they are aware of the narrow standard of beauty too. And it's easy to accept the standard as truth, especially when it is supported by those closest to you. Here's how I know.

THE BLACK WOMAN'S BODY IMAGE DIET

For most of my life my mother worked at a bank, which I learned through snickers and sneers from members of our community was a "sit down job." I also learned that it was the opinion of some that my mother's position at such a job was somehow related to the fact that she was fair-skinned with long hair. My great grandmother who was well into her eighties at the time would compliment my mom when she'd come home from work wearing huge square, wire rimmed glasses and her loose curls resting on her shoulders. Always, she was dressed smartly in a blouse usually with a bow tied neatly at the neck, thin belt, full skirt, hose and heels. My great-grandmother would say, "Oh, honey, you look so pretty today, so pretty, just like a little white lady!"

Of course, from my great grandmother's perspective, this was the highest form of compliment and it was delivered in just that manner. In response, my mother would simply smile, nod and say thank you. Though the weight of those words may never be known for sure, for this little Black girl, the message spoke volumes.

That lesson was not lost on me. Today I am the proud aunt of an amazing 21-year-old niece. She is a beautiful woman inside and out. She loves life and her little brother, summertime, and sunny days. She's polite and kind, gentle and sweet, and when she was young, I made it a point to tell her often that she was smart and beautiful. I did this with an array of compliments that included aesthetics but also with many more that did not. I complimented her so much because I feared that otherwise one day, out in the real world, she might be made to feel anything other than the wonderful person she was because of her size or

MELINDA GORE

her complexion or something else that didn't matter. This is why it is more important than ever to spread the word about body positive living. Our young women are looking to us, the adults, to be examples. Remember earlier you learned that daughters of body-dissatisfied mothers are likely to become dissatisfied with their bodies too. Our young women deserve better than that, so it is our job to change the message and the world. We owe it to them as well as ourselves to give them something more.

As we have already discussed in this book, starting a conversation about body positive living is not just for the benefit of young women and girls. This conversation is for everyone. It's for our sons who will one day be faced with the decision to accept or reject the narrow standards of beauty that define what an ideal girlfriend should look like. It's for fathers who need to arm themselves with information so they are able to engage in meaningful conversations with sons and daughters about the importance of positive body image. It's for husbands who must learn to communicate with wives in ways that foster body positivity. It's for women who have recently moved beyond their teen years only to find themselves as young adults who are unrealistically critical of their bodies as a result of the media's unrealistic beauty standards. It's for women beyond their twenties like you and me who never learned to appreciate our bodies when we were younger. It's for women entering their fifties and sixties who must find beauty, appreciation, and acceptance in aging bodies. I applaud any effort that is being made to encourage people of all ages, shapes, shades, sizes, and sexes to see themselves more positively, but it is up to each of us individually to change negative messages.

I understand that the steps in this book may take some time to integrate into your daily life. I also acknowledge that no one thing on its own will exclude any of us from ever having issues with negative body image again. However, what I do know is that by incorporating what you have learned, one step at a time, you will move closer to creating an environment for body-positive living.

Your challenge as you continue to grow and move forward is to take what you have learned about body positive living, not just as additional information, but to adopt it as a way of life (*diaita*). However, do not stop there. Do not be tempted to keep it to yourself; instead vow to be the change you want to see in the world. Show the world some of that Black Girl Magic! Now that you can change the way you feel about the reflection in the mirror, you can help others do the same. The time is now. We've seen the damaging effects of the one-sided images in the media. Let's not stand by and wait for change to take place; let's do it together and make it happen. I would love to see clubs, sororities, and other groups of women work together to spread the word about body positive living.

So, what can you do?

GIVE COMPLIMENTS

Today, tell someone how beautiful you think they are on the inside and the outside. Use compliments that are not limited to aesthetics. Look for beauty in others using your newly expanded definition of beauty and encourage others to do the same.

MELINDA GORE

CELEBRATE INDIVIDUALITY

Make it a point to celebrate differences and unique qualities in yourself as well as in others. Make the effort to keep comparisons to a minimum. When they do show up, extend compassion to yourself and others.

START A CONVERSATION

Encourage conversations with your friends, in person or on social media. How about this for an opener: "What do you think makes a woman beautiful?" Then, depending upon the response, follow up with a question such as, "If that's what 'beautiful' means to you, have you ever considered all the kinds of women you're leaving out?" Post a question to your social media. Get people talking about this topic and see what others have to say.

KEEP LEARNING

By all means, keep learning. Check out other books about positive body image. Find blogs that inspire you to see yourself more positively. Arm yourself with as much information as possible. And don't forget to share what you learn with those around you.

THE BLACK WOMAN'S BODY IMAGE DIET

We are at the end of the book but only the beginning of the journey. You've been given valuable new information to include in your arsenal to develop the art of body positive living. Let's recap:

Step One: *Create Your Own Definition of Beauty*. With a newly created, more inclusive definition of beauty, you can begin to admire those wonderful things in yourself and encourage others to do the same.

Step Two: *Avoid Unhealthy Messages.* Odds are that many unwanted messages will continue to show up in your life. But you now have the tools and information you need to determine which messages you will allow in and which ones you will delete without wavering.

Step Three: *Don't Compare Apples to Oranges.* A major part of body positive living is a greater appreciation for yourself and your own journey. Now that you are aware of how comparisons may be keeping you from seeing yourself more positively, you are prepared to find new ways of appreciating your uniqueness and celebrating individuality.

Step Four: *Choose Your Thoughts.* You can't stop thoughts from coming, but you can manage your reaction to them. With new tools like thought interruption, positive self-talk, reframing, and visualization, you are armed with powerful ammunition to protect yourself from those negative thoughts that try to disrupt body positive living.

MELINDA GORE

Step Five: Engage in Joyful Movement. Your discovery and adoption of personalized joyful movement is an important step toward bringing about a long-lasting change in your physical activity. In addition to the multitude of health benefits that come along with movement, body positive living can be yours as well.

Step Six: Eat Feel-Good Foods. Food is a big part of all our lives, and you now have all the tools you need to make your food work for you. Get busy taking full advantage of mood-boosting power in every bite. Try out a few delicious new recipes and snack ideas to inspire you to eat well and feel well for a long time to come.

Step Seven: Express Your Spirituality. With prayer, meditation, and journaling, you are well equipped to express your spirituality and extend greater love and acceptance for your body.

Step Eight: Keep Your Friends Close and Those Who Encourage You Closer. Body positive living thrives with the support of positive and safe social circles. Avoid friends who engage in "fat talk" and other self-deprecating behavior and seek friends who uplift your spirits.

Step Nine: Create a Healthy Haven. You are prepared to create and design your own healthy haven with purposeful paint, appropriate lighting, cozy fabrics, inspirational art, and so much more.

THE BLACK WOMAN'S BODY IMAGE DIET

Step Ten: Pamper Yourself to Enhance Your Health and Beauty. You now see why self-care is the frosting on the cake. You understand that an artful balance of healthy living along with self-care beauty practices is essential. With great health and beauty ideas, you can practice adornment as a means of expression, self-care, and self-elevation.

All of these steps taken together and personalized to suit you will lead you to a body positive way of life, an artful blend of mind, body, and spirit. With every bit of new information you have gained, you are better equipped to fend off any negative messages about your body that come your way. That's the power of feeling good about yourself, something Michelle Obama says her father tried to instill in her at an early age. When she was young, he often reminded her, "No one can make you feel bad if you feel good about yourself." Now, as a middle-aged Black woman, she recalls, "It took me years to absorb my dad's maxim more fully into my own life. I grew into my confidence slowly, in fits and starts. Only gradually did I learn to carry my differentness with pride."[195] So celebrate your "differentness." Love the body that is uniquely yours. Then, like Michelle Obama, share your story. Spread the word and change the world!

ACKNOWLEDGEMENTS

Thank you to everyone who made this book possible, especially my family for always being so supportive of all my endeavors.

To my mother Maralyn, your relentless encouragement always made me feel beautiful inside and out and capable of anything, especially during my awkward tween years when I was super self-conscious about my body. Somehow you always found the right words to make everything ok. Thanks mom.

To my sisters Stephanie and Amy. Sisters are indeed the best kind of friends. Thank you both for being such extraordinary examples of beautiful, bold, confident Black women.

To the many clients I've had the pleasure of working with over the years who truly squeezed this message out of me. I greatly appreciate you all.

Many thanks to all the people who have given their expertise to make this book a wonderful work of art that I am so proud to share.

To Teresa Redd, my God-send of an editor, thank you for lending your wisdom, going above and beyond and for believing in me and this message.

MELINDA GORE

Thank you Pinodesk for the most beautiful illustrations adding just the right sentiment to every chapter.

Finally, I want to extend a special thank you to every Black woman who has been an inspiration in my life throughout the years. Many of you I have never met, but I am hopeful that one day I will. Your way of being in the world has given me the ability to dream the impossible dreams.

Thank you, Oprah Winfrey, Former First Lady Michelle Obama, Vice President Kamala Harris, Beyonce, Gayle King, Viola Davis, Nischelle Turner, Tracee Ellis Ross, Tabitha Brown, Issa Rae, Regina King, Tonya Lewis Lee, Renae Bluitt, Sheinelle Jones, Tonya Rapley, Ananda Lewis, Elaine Welteroth, Tyra Banks, Shonda Rhimes, Quinta Brunson, Vanessa Williams, Donna Richardson, Tamron Hall, Starr Jones, Marshawn Daniels, Lisa Nichols, Kelly Roland, and Melissa Butler. The list could easily go on and on. Thank you all!!

Endnotes

1. JJ Chinn, IK Martin, N Redmond, "Health Equity Among Black Women in the United States." *Journal of Women's Health* vol. 30,2 (2021): 212-219. doi:10.1089/jwh.2020.8868.

2. See the infographic at https://www.glossy.co/beauty/dove-funds-new-report-showing-beauty-standards-are-a-public-health-crisis/.

3. Kay Uzoma, "Percentage of Americans who diet every year," *Livestrong*.com, 2017.

4. S Grogan, *Body Image: Understanding Body Dissatisfaction in Men, Women and Children* (New York: Routledge, 2017).

5. Jess Sims, "Dear Fat, Black Girls Who Were Not Spared from Diet Culture – I Understand," *Healthline*, July 8, 2022, https://www.health-line.com/health/diet-culture-affects-fat-black-women

6. R Dotinga, "The average Americans' weight change since the 1980s is startling," *CBS News*, August 3, 2016, https://www.cbsnews.com/news/americans-weight-gain-since-1980s-startling/

7. Grogan, *Body Image: Understanding Body Dissatisfaction in Men, Women and Children.*

8. J Juhaeri et al, "Weight change among self-reported dieters and non-dieters in white and African American men and women," *European Journal of Epidemiology*, 17(10) (2001): 917–23.

9. ML Fitzgibbon, LM Tussing-Humphreys, JS Porter et al, "Weight loss and African-American women: a systematic review of the behavioural weight loss intervention literature," *Obes Rev.* 13(3) (March 2012):193–213.

10. C.D Runfola, A.V. Holle, S.E. Trace et al, "Body dissatisfaction in women across the lifespan: results of the UNC-SELF and gender and body image (GABI) studies," *European Eating Disorders Review, 21*, (2013): 52–59.

11. Stronge, et al, "Facebook is linked to body dissatisfaction: comparing users and non-users," *Sex Roles, 73* (2015):200–213.

12. G.H. Awad, C. Norwood, DS Taylor et al, "Beauty and Body Image Concerns Among African American College Women," *J Black Psychol.* 41(6) (December 2015):540–564. Epub Nov 12 2014.

13   *The Merriam-Webster Dictionary.*

14   diaita. (n.1). Retrieved August 12, 2018, from Online Etymology Dictionary, www.etymonline.com.

15   Grogan, *Body Image: Understanding Body Dissatisfaction in Men, Women and Children.*

16   FitzSimons-Craft et al, "The Relationships among Social Comparisons, Body Surveillance, and Body Dissatisfaction in the Natural Environment," *Behavior Therapy, 45* (2015): 257-271.

17   C. Martijn, J.M Alleva & A. Jansen, "Improving Body Satisfaction: Do Strategies Targeting Automatic Systems Work?" *European Psychologist, 20*(1) (2015): 62–71.

18   J. Mond, D. Mitchison, J. Latner et al. "Quality of life impairment associated with body dissatisfaction in general population sample of women," *BMC Public Health* 13, 920 (2013); Better Health Channel Body Image – women, *Betterhealth.vic.gov.au.*

19   See Dove's report downloaded from https://www.dove.com/us/en/stories/campaigns/real-cost-of-beauty/thestats.html. Diagram on page 51.

20   Amanda Nussbaum, "Body 'Zoom' Dysmorphia – The Impact Zoom has on Body Image," *Balance*, December, 2021, https://balancedtx.com/blog/body-zoomdysmorphia-the-impact-zoom-has-on-body-image#:~:text=Although%20a%20person%20with%20BDD,about%20is%20seen%20and%20visible

21   A. Slater & M. Tiggemann, "A test of objectification in adolescent girls," *Sex Roles, 46* (2002):343–349.

22   Grogan, *Body Image: Understanding Body Dissatisfaction in Men, Women and Children.*

23   Katherine Lee, "6 Ways to Help Young Children Avoid Body Image Issues," *VeryWell*, May, 2022, https://www.verywellfamily.com/ways-to-help-young-children-avoid-body-image-issues-4114718.

24   Martijn et al, "Improving body satisfaction: do strategies targeting automatic systems work?" 62–71.

25   Martijn et al, "Improving body satisfaction: do strategies targeting automatic systems work?" 62–71.

26   Runfola, et al, "Characteristics of women with body size satisfaction at midlife: results of the gender and body image study," *Journal of Women & Aging, 25* (2013): 287–304.

27   Runfola, et al, "Characteristics of women with body size satisfaction at midlife: results of the gender and body image study," 287–304.

28 T. Tylka & N. Wood-Barcalow, "A Positive Complement," *Body Image, 14* (2015): 115 -17.

29 Runfola, et al, "Characteristics of women with body size satisfaction at midlife: results of the gender and body image study," 287–304.

30 Grogan, *Body Image: Understanding Body Dissatisfaction in Men, Women and Children.*

31 T.F. Cash & T. Pruzinsky, *Future challenges for body image theory, research, and clinical practice. In: Cash, T.F., Pruzinsky T. Body Image* (New York : Guilford Press, 2002).

32 J. Rodin, L. Silberstein & R. Striegel-Moore, "Women and weight: A normative discontent," in T.B. Sonderegger (Ed.), *Psychology and gender* (Lincoln: University of Nebraska Press, 1985) 267–307.

33 R. Engeln, *Beauty Sick: How the Cultural Obsession with Appearance Hurts Girls and Women* (New York: HarperCollins, 2017).

34 R. Stokes & C. Frederick-Recascino, "Women's Perceived Body Image: Relations with Personal Happiness," *Journal of Women and Aging, 15* (2003): 17–29.

35 S. M. Hofmeier, C. D Runfola, M. Sala et al, "Body image, aging, and identity in women over 50: the gender and body image (GABI) study," *Journal of Women & Aging, 29*(1) (2017): 3–14.

36 Anderson, et al, "Relationship of satisfaction with body size and trying to lose weight in a national survey of overweight and obese women aged 40 and older," *Preventative Medicine, 35* (4) (2002): 390–396.

37 N.A.R Wood & T. A. Petrie, "Body Dissatisfaction, Ethnic Identity, and Disordered Eating Among African American Women," *Journal of Counseling Psychology, 57* (2) (2010): 141–153.

38 Fallon et al. (2014) cited in Dove report: https://cdn1.sph.harvard. edu/wp-content/uploads/sites/1267/2022/10/Real-Cost-of-Beauty-Report-10-4-22.pdf

39 Dawnie Walton, "Essence's Images Study: Bonus Insights," *Essence.com*, October, 2020, https://www.essence.com/lifestyle/essence-images-study-bonus-insights/

40 Virginia Ramseyer Winter, Laura King Danforth, Antoinette Landor, Danielle Pevehouse-Pfeiffer, "Toward an Understanding of Racial and Ethnic Diversity in Body Image among Women," *Social Work Research*, Volume 43, Issue 2 (June 2019): 69–80.

41 Tatiana Walk-Morris, "How Eurocentric Beauty Standards Harm Black Women," *Shape.com*, November 9, 2021; Navya Varma, "The Effects of the Eurocentric Beauty Standards on Women of Color," *GenZHer*, May 2, 2021; Leah Donella, "Is Beauty in the eyes of the colonizer?" *Ask Code Switch Podcast, NPR*, Feb 6, 2019.

42 N.L., Wood-Barcalow, T.L. Tylka & C.L. Augustus-Horvath, "But I like my body: positive body image characteristics and a holistic model for young-adult women," *Body Image: An International Journal of Research, 7* (2010): 106–116.

43 "Healthy Body Image Quiz: 11 Questions to establish Your Level of Body Positivity," *Askthescientists.com*.

44 M.P. Levine, "Media influences on female body image," in T.F. Cash (Ed.) *Encyclopedia of body image and human appearance* (London: Elsevier, 2012) 540–6.

45 *Merriam Webster Dictionary.*

46 L. Smolak, "Body Image in Children and Adolescents: Where Do We Go From Here," *Body Image, 1*(1) (2004): 15–28.

47 See the Dove campaign at: https://www.dove.com/us/en/stories/campaigns.html; the Dove October 2022 report "The Real Cost of Beauty Ideals" is available at: https://www.dove.com/content/dam/unilever/dove/global/brand_essentials_and_toolkits/dove_report_digital_assessment_01-89405289.pdf.

48 Available at: https://www.vogue.co.uk/article/british-vogue-loreal-paris-present-the-non-issue-issue

49 Available at: https://www.usmagazine.com/celebrity-body/pictures/every-time-lizzo-preached-body-positivity-photos/

50 Amy Roeder, "Advertising's toxic effect on eating and body image," Harvard.com News, March, 2015, https://www.hsph.harvard.edu/news/features/advertisings-toxic-effect-on-eating-and-body-image/

51 L. Smolak, "Body image in children and adolescents: where do we go from here?" *Body Image, 1* (1) (2004): 15–28.

52 T. Cruwys, C. Leverington & A. Sheldon, "An experimental investigation of the consequences and social functions of fat talk in friendship groups," *International Journal of Eating Disorders* 49 (2016); 84–91.

53 S. M. Hofmeier, C. D. Runfola, M. Sala, M et al, "Body image, aging, and identity in women over 50: the gender and body image (GABI) study," 3–14.

54 Rowina Debalkew, "Breaking Down the Stereotypes: Celebrating the Black Woman," *The Women's Network*, March, 2022, https://www.thewomens.network/blog/breaking-down-the-stereotypes-celebrating-the-black-woman

55 Robin Givhan, "Dangerous Beauty," The Washington Post, October, 2022, https://www.washingtonpost.com/nation/2022/10/18/dangerous-beauty/

56 Adele Jackson-Gibson, "The Racist and Problematic History of the Body Mass Index," Good Housekeeping, February, 2021, https://www.goodhousekeeping.com/health/diet-nutrition/a35047103/bmi-racist-history/; Sabrina Strings, "The Racist Roots of Fighting Obesity," *Scientific American*, June, 2021, https://www.scientificamerican.com/article/the-racist-roots-of-fighting-obesity2/

57 S. Stronge et al, "Facebook is linked to body dissatisfaction: Comparing users and non-users," 200–213.

58 Grogan, *Body Image: Understanding Body Dissatisfaction in Men, Women and Children.*

59 S. Bordo, *"Unbearable Weight: Feminism, Western Culture, and the Body,"* 10th anniversary edition (Berkley, CA: University of California Press, 2003).

60 Martijn et al, "Improving body satisfaction: do strategies targeting automatic systems work?" 62–71.

61 P. Diedrichs & C. Lee, "Waif goodbye! Average-size female models promote positive body image and appeal to consumers," *Psychology and Health, 26*(10) (2011): 1273-1291.

62 E. E. FitzSimons-Craft et al, "The Relationships among Social Comparisons, Body Surveillance, and Body Dissatisfaction in the Natural Environment," 257-271.

63 E. Strahan, A. Wilson, K. Cressman & V. Buote, "Comparing to perfection: how cultural norms for appearance affect social comparisons and self-image," *Body Image, 3* (2006): 211-227.

64 Compare. 2018. In *Merriam-Webster.com.* Retrieved August 12, 2018, from https://www.merriam webster.com/dictionary/compare

65 B. McHugh, "The Desperate Housewives Effect," Families.com, January, 2006. Retrieved from http://mental-health.families.com/blog/thedesperatehousewiveseffect; J. Pannasch, "Study shows midlife eating disorders on the rise," *MSNBC Interactive*, March, 2008. Retrieved from today.com.

66 V. Hefner et al, "The Influence of Television and Film Viewing on Midlife Women's Body Image, Disordered Eating, and Food Choice," *Media Psychology, 17* (2014): 185–207.

67 J.K. Thompson, P. van den Berg, M. Roehrig et al, "The sociocultural attitudes towards appearance scale-3: development and validation," *International Journal of Eating Disorders, 35* (2004): 293–304.

68 Bordo, *Unbearable weight: Feminism, Western culture, and the Body.*

69 L. Festinger, "A Theory of Social Comparison Processes," *Human Relations, 7* (1954): 117–140.

70 L. Lin & J. Kulik, "Social Comparison and Women's Body Satisfaction," *Basic and Applied Social Psychology, 24* (2002): 115–123.

71 K. Watts, J. Cranney & M. Gleitzman, "Automatic Evaluation of Body-related Images," *Body Image, 5* (2008): 352-364.

72 T. M. Leahey, J. H. Crowther & K. D. Mickelson, "The Frequency, Nature, and Effects of Naturally Occurring Appearance-focused Social Comparisons," *Behavior Therapy, 38* (2007): 132–143.

73 S. Stronge et al, "Facebook is linked to body dissatisfaction: Comparing users and non-users," 200–213.

74 S. Stronge et al, "Facebook is linked to body dissatisfaction: Comparing users and non-users," 200–213.

75 S. Stronge et al, "Facebook is linked to body dissatisfaction: Comparing users and non-users," 200–213.

76 Robin Givhan, "Dangerous Beauty."

77 K. Neff, "Self-compassion," in ed. Mark Leary and Rick Hoyle, *Handbook of Individual Differences in Social Behavior* (New York: Guilford Press, 2009).

78 C. Sobczak, *Embody: Learning to Love your Unique Body and Quiet that Critical Voice!* (Carlsbad: Gurze Books, 2014).

79 R. Engeln, *Beauty Sick: How the Cultural Obsession with Appearance Hurts Girls and Women.*

80 D.M. Lewis & F.M. Cachelin, "Body image, body dissatisfaction, and eating attitudes in midlife and elderly women," *Eating Disorders, 9* (2001): 29-39; M.A. Gupta, "Fear of aging: a precipitating factor in late onset anorexia nervosa," *International Journal of Eating Disorders, 9* (1990): 221-224.

81 L. Pridgeon and S. Grogan, "Understanding exercise adherence and dropout: An interpretive phenomenological analysis of men's and women's accounts of gym attendance and non-attendance," *Qualitative Research in Sport, Exercise and Health, 4*(3) (2012): 382–99.

82   International Society of Aesthetic Plastic Surgery, *Global Statistics*, 2015, available online at www.isaps.org.

83   The Aesthetic Society, "The Aesthetic Society Releases Annual Statistics Revealing Significant Increases in Face, Breast and Body in 2021," *PR Newswire.com*, April 11, 2022, https://www.prnews-wire.com/news-releases/the-aesthetic-society-releases-annual-statistics-revealing-significant-increases-in-face-breast-and-body-in-2021-301522417.html

84   See the Plastic Surgery Statistics Report at https://www.plasticsur-gery.org/documents/News/Statistics/2020/cosmetic-procedures-ethnicity-2020.pdf.

85   Abby Ellin, "Brazilian Butt Lifts Surge, despite Risks," *The New York Times*, August 19, 2021, https://www.nytimes.com/2021/08/19/style/brazillian-butt-lift-bbl-how-much-risks.html

86   C. Sobczak, *Embody: Learning to Love your Unique Body and Quiet that Critical Voice!*

87   Association for Size Diversity and Health: www.sizediversityand-health.org

88   Sobczak, *Embody: Learning to Love your Unique Body and Quiet that Critical Voice!*

89   T.F. Cash, B.A. Winstead and L.H. Janda, "The great American shape-up: body image survey report," *Psychology Today, 20* (1986): 20-37.

90   Jean Williams, *Applied Sport Psychology: Personal Growth to Peak Performance* (New York: McGraw Hill, 2006).

91   G.A. Brooks, N.F. Butte, W.M. Rand et al, "Chronicle of the institute of medicine physical activity recommendation: how a physical activity recommendation came to be among dietary recommendations," *The American Journal of Clinical Nutrition, 79*(5) (2004): 921–930.

92   Yvette Brazier, "Muscles: Why are they important?" *Medical News Today*, April 25, 2021.

93   K.A. Martin Ginis, R.L. Bassett-Gunter and C. Conlin, "Body image and exercise," in E.O. Acevedo (Ed.), *Oxford Handbook of Exercise Psychology* (Oxford: Oxford University Press, 2012) 55–75.

94   K.A. Martin Ginis et al, "The effects of aerobic versus strength train-ing on body image among young women with pre-existing body image concerns," *Body Image, 11* (2014): 219–227.

95   Mayo Clinic Staff, "Exercise and stress: Get moving to manage stress," *Mayo Clinic*. Retrieved from www.mayoclinic.org August 13, 2018.

96 "Exercise for stress and anxiety," *Anxiety and Depression Association of America*. Retrieved from www.adaa.org.

97 A.T. Geronimus et al, "Black women experience stress-related accelerated biological aging? A novel theory and first population-based test of black-white differences in telomere length," *Hum Nat* 21 (2010):19–38 cited in Chinn et al, "Health Equity Among Black Women in the United States."

98 Mayo Clinic Staff, "Aerobic Exercise: Top 10 reasons to get physical," *Mayo Clinic*.

99 The World Health Organization: www.who.int.

100 Office of Minority Health, "Profile: Black/African Americans," *HHS.gov*, https://www.minorityhealth.hhs.gov/omh/browse.aspx?lvl=3&lvlid=61

101 M. Moore, E. Jackson and B. Tschannen-Moran, *Wellcoaches Coaching Psychology Manual* (Wolters Kluwer, Pennyslvania, 2016).

102 C. Sobczak, *Embody: Learning to Love your Unique Body and Quiet that Critical Voice!*

103 W. M. Williams, M.M. Yore, M. C. Whitt-Glover, "Estimating physical activity trends among blacks in the United States through examination of four national surveys," *AIMS Public Health* 5(2) (May 29 2018):144–157.

104 R. Hall, S. Francis, M. Whitt-Glover and K. Loftin-Bell, "Hair care practices as a barrier to physical activity in African American Women," *JAMA Dermatol* 149(3) (March 2013):310–14.

105 "How to Protect Your Hair From Sweat While Working Out," *Sweat*: https://www.sweat.com/blogs/life/is-sweating-good-for-your-hair

106 www.mysunday2sunday.com

107 www.gymwrap.com

108 www.soulcap.com

109 K.A. Martin Ginis et al, "The effects of aerobic versus strength training on body image among young women with pre-existing body image concerns," 219–227.

110 The World Health Organization: www.who.int

111 A. Campbell and H.A. Hausenblas, "Effects of exercise interventions on body image: a meta-analysis," *Journal of Health Psychology, 14* (2009): 1–14.

112 P. Afshari, Z. Houshyar, N. Javadifar et al, "The Relationship Between Body Image and Sexual Function in Middle-Aged Women," *Electron Physician* 25;8(11) (Nov 2016):3302–3308; "Is Body Image Affecting

Your Sex Life? Resolve to free sex from the critical inner voice," *Psychology Today.*

113 Laurie J. Waston, PhD, "Is Body Image Affecting Your Sex Life? Resolve to free sex from the critical inner voice." *Psychology Today,* December 2018.

114 R.H. Striegel-Moore, D.E. Wilfley, K.M. Pike et al, "Recurrent binge eating in black American women," *Arch Fam Med.* 9(1) (2009): 83–87.

115 US Department of Health and Human services at minorityhealth. hhs.gov – Obesity and African Americans; Chinn et al, "Health Equity Among Black Women in the United States."

116 C. Merryfield, "Confidence and self-esteem," *Nutritionist Resource,* Web. May, 2017.

117 J. Gangwisch, L. Hale, L. Garcia et al, "High glycemic index diet as a risk factor for depression: analyses from the women's health initiative," *The American Journal of Clinical Nutrition, 102* (2) (2015): 454–463.

118 Office of Minority Health, "Mental and Behavioral Health – African Americans," *HHS.gov,* https://minorityhealth.hhs.gov/omh/browse. aspx?lvl=4&lvlid=24

119 T.S. Conner, K.L., Brooke, A.C. Carr et al, "Let them eat fruit! The effect of fruit and vegetable consumption on psychological well-being in young adults: A randomized controlled trial," *Plos One 12*(2) (2017): 1–19.

120 A. Haupt, "Food and mood. 6 ways your diet affects how you feel," *US News,* August 31, 2011. Retrieved from http://www.usnews.com.

121 C. Merryfield, "Confidence and self-esteem."

122 A. Haupt, "Food and mood. 6 ways your diet affects how you feel."

123 E. Magee, "How food affects your moods," *WebMD,* December 15, 2009. Retrieved from http://www.webmd.com.

124 D. Benon and R. Donohoe, "The effects of nutrients on mood," *Public Health Nutrition, 2*(3A) (1999): 403–9.

125 E. Magee, "How food affects your moods."

126 Cordialis Msora-Kasag, "How to Create a Healthy Soul Food Plate," Healthline, February, 2021, https://www.healthline.com/nutrition/ healthy-soul-food#bottom-line

127 Examples: "Healthy Soul Food Recipes," *EatingWell,* https://www.eatingwell.com/recipes/19700/cuisines-regions/usa/soul/; Alice Randall and Caroline Randall Williams, Soul Food Love (New York: Clarkson Potter, 2015).

128 E. Magee, "How food affects your moods."

129 Fatima Hallal, "When Should You Stop Eating at Night," Healthline, July, 2021, https://www.healthline.com/nutrition/what-time-should-you-stop-eating#recommendation

130 "Better food, better mood: Is Your Diet Affecting Your Mental Health," *Providence.org.* July 2022.

131 Yvette Brazier, "Muscles: Why are they important?" *Medical News Today*, April 25, 2021.

132 H.G. Koenig, M.E. McCullough, D.B. Larson, *Handbook of Religion and Health* (New York: Oxford University Press, 2001).

133 L.K. George, D.B. Larson, H.G. Koenig and M.E. McCulough, "Spirituality and health: What we know, what we need to know," *Journal of Social and Clinical Psychology, 19* (2000): 102–116.

134 J. Lundstad, P.R. Steffen, J. Sandberg and B. Jensen, "Understanding the connection between spiritual well-being and physical health: an examination of ambulatory blood pressure, blood lipids and fasting glucose," *Journal of Behavioral Medicine, 34* (2011): 477–488.

135 well-being. (n.d.). Retrieved May 10, 2017, from https://www.merri-am-webster.com/dictionary/well-being

136 M. Moore, E. Jackson and B. Tschannen-Moran, *Wellcoaches Coaching Psychology.*

137 National Cancer Institute, "Spirituality," in *Dictionary of Cancer Terms.* Available at http://www.cancer.gov.

138 D.B. Larsen, J.P. Swyers and M.E. McCullough, *Scientific Research on Spirituality and Health. A Consensus Report* (Rockville, MD: National Institute for Healthcare Research, 1997).

139 P. Love, D. Talbot, "Defining spiritual development: a missing consideration for student affairs," *Journal of Student Affairs Research and Practice, 37* (1999): 361–376.

140 Roxanne A. Donovan and Lindsay M. West, "Stress and Mental Health: Moderating Role of the Strong Black Woman Stereotype," *Journal of Black Psychology* Volume 41, Issue 4 (August 2015): 384–396.

141 K. J. Homan and C. J. Boyatzis, "The protective role of attachment to God against eating disorder risk factors: Concurrent and prospective evidence," *Eating Disorders: The Journal of Treatment and Prevention, 18* (2010): 1–20; K. J. Homan, "Attachment to God mitigates negative effect of media exposure on women's body image," *Psychology of Religion and Spirituality, 4* (2012): 324–331.

142 C.J. Boyatzis, S. Kline and S. Backof, "Experimental evidence that theistic-religious body affirmations improve women's body image," *Journal for the Scientific Study of Religion, 46* (2007): 553–564; A. Mahoney, R.A. Carels, K.I Pargament et al, "The sanctification of the body and behavioral health patterns of college students," *International Journal for the Psychology of Religion, 15* (2005): 221–238.

143 M.J. Jacobs-Pilipski, A. Winzelberg, D.E. Wilfey et al, "Spirituality among young women at risk for eating disorders," *Eating Behaviors, 6* (2005): 293–300.

144 C.J. Boyatzis, M. McConnell, "Females' religious and spiritual well-being, body esteem, and eating disorders." Paper presented at the meeting of the *American Psychological Association*, Chicago, 2002.

145 C.J. Boyatzis, S. Kline and S. Backof, "Experimental evidence that theistic-religious body affirmations improve women's body image," 553–564

146 J. House, K. Landis and D. Umberson, "Social Relationships and Health," *Science, 241* (1988): 540-544.

147 A. Young, S. Gabriel and O. Schlager, "Does this friend make me look fat? Appearance-related comparisons within women's close friendships," *Basic and Applied Social Psychology, 36* (2014): 145–154.

148 A. Young, S. Gabriel and O. Schlager, "Does this friend make me look fat? Appearance-related comparisons within women's close friendships."

149 Martijn et al, "Improving body satisfaction: do strategies targeting automatic systems work?" 62–71.

150 T. Cruwys, C. Leverington and A. Sheldon, "An experimental investigation of the consequences and social functions of fat talk in friendship groups," *International Journal of Eating Disorders, 49* (2016): 84–91.

151 T. Cruwys, C. Leverington and A. Sheldon, "An experimental investigation of the consequences and social functions of fat talk in friendship groups."

152 Tishanna Renee Hollins, "Fat Talk Among Caucasian and African American Women," *Faculty of the College of Arts and Sciences of American University*, 2011, https://dra.american.edu/islandora/object/thesesdissertations%3A248; Mallory F Fiery et al, "A preliminary investigation of racial differences in body talk in age-diverse U.S. adults." *Eating Behaviors* vol. 21 (2016): 232–5.

153 Lenora Goodman, "Changing the Culture Around Fat-Talk," School of Public Health, May 23, 2018, https://sph.umich.edu/pursuit/2018posts/changing-the-culture-around-fat-talk.html

154 President and Fellows of Harvard College, "Harvard Heart Letter," *Harvard Health Publications*, Copyright 2018.

155 A. Christen, "Neuroarchitecture: home design for your mood," *Hello Life*, December 7, 2012. Retrieved from https://www.smartlivingnetwork.com

156 J. Corkery, "Boost Your Mood Using 5 Scientific Decorating Tips," *WIMDU*, September 10, 2015. Retrieved from wimdu.co.uk

157 J. Farley, "Neuroarchitecture: The New Movement at the Forefront of Design," *Houzz*, May 28, 2018. Retrieved from houzz.com.au.

158 J. Eberhard, "Applying neuroscience to architecture," *Neuron, 62*(6) (2009): 753–756.

159 Pattinson Professional Counseling and Mediation Center, October 24, 2016. Retrieved from http://www.ppccfl.com

160 Jaymes Dempsey, "How to get the best lighting for your portrait photography," *PhotoWorkout*, July, 2022, https://www.photoworkout.com/portrait-photography-lighting/

161 Photofeeler, "How Lighting Changes What You Look Like," *Photofeeler*, April, 2020, https://blog.photofeeler.com/lighting/

162 Alex Williams, "Why Does Fluorescent Lighting Make You Look Bad?" *Speeli.com*, April, 2022, https://www.speeli.com/why-does-fluorescent-lighting-make-you-look-bad/

163 Sarah Garone, "The Health Benefits of Natural Light," *Healthline*, August, 2020, https://www.healthline.com/health/natural-light-benefits#benefits

164 C. Obenschain, "Can the color of a room affect your mood?" *How Stuff Works*, December 6, 2010. Retrieved from howstuffworks.com

165 C. Obenschain, "Can the color of a room affect your mood?"

166 A. Christen, "Neuroarchitecture: Home design for your mood," *Hello Life*, December 7, 2012. Retrieved from https://www.smartlivingnetwork.com.

167 Luanne Bradley, "Neuroarchitecture: The Science of Getting Your Décor in the Right Frame of Mind," *Ecosalon*, July 10, 2009. Retrieved from ecosalon.com.

168 The Daily Dish, "Neuro-Architecture," *The Atlantic*, October 13, 2007. Retrieved from https://www.theatlantic.com

169 J. Corkery, "Boost Your Mood Using 5 Scientific Decorating Tips."

170 J. Corkery, "Boost Your Mood Using 5 Scientific Decorating Tips."

171 Tanck, Julia A, Andrea Sabrina Hartmann, Jennifer Svaldi and Silja Vocks. "Effects of full-body mirror exposure on eating pathology, body image and emotional states: Comparison between positive and negative verbalization." *PLoS ONE* 16 (2021): n. pag.

172 Jari Roomer, "Science Says Decluttering Your Work Environment Improves Your Focus & Productivity," *Medium.com*, June, 2019, https://medium.com/personal-growth-lab/science-says-decluttering-your-work-environment-improves-your-focus-productivity-f2ca317f689c

173 M. Moore, E. Jackson and B. Tschannen-Moran, *Wellcoaches Coaching Psychology.*

174 R. Engeln, *Beauty Sick: How the Cultural Obsession with Appearance Hurts Girls and Women.*

175 Nielsen, "African American Spending Power Demands that Marketers Show More Love and Support for Black Culture," *Nielsen*, September, 2019, https://www.nielsen.com/news-center/2019/african-american-spending-power-demands-that-marketers-show-more-love-and-support-for-black-culture/

176 www.blackgirlsunscreen.com

177 Emma K T Benn et al, "Skin Bleaching Among African and Afro-Caribbean Women in New York City: Primary Findings from a P30 Pilot Study." *Dermatology and therapy* vol. 9,2 (2019): 355–367; Maya Allen, "The Reality of Skin Bleaching and the History Behind It," *Byrdie*, updated May, 2022, https://www.byrdie.com/skin-bleaching.

178 Tayo Bero, "Black women's hair products are killing us. Why isn't more being done?" *The Guardian*, July, 2021, https://www.theguardian.com/commentisfree/2021/jul/27/black-women-hair-products-health-hazards-study.

179 www.urbanhydration.com.

180 "The Truth About Dry Brushing and What It Does for You," *Cleveland Clinic.* November, 2021, https://health.clevelandclinic.org/the-truth-about-dry-brushing-and-what-it-does-for-you/

181 Funmi Fetto, "How Fenty Beauty Changed the State of Play in the Industry," *Vogue*, April, 2020, https://www.vogue.co.uk/beauty/article/rihanna-fenty-beauty-diversity

182 www.fashionfair.com.

183 Victoria Stanell, "Bobby Brown gets pretty real on confidence," *BeautyLish*, October, 2021, https://www.beautylish.com/a/vcqvi/bobbi-brown-gets-pretty-real-on-confidence

184 Dove, "The Real Cost of Beauty Ideals," October, 2022, https://www.dove.com/content/dam/unilever/dove/global/brand_essentials_and_toolkits/dove_report_digital_assessment_01-89405289.pdf

185 Tayo Bero, "Black women's hair products are killing us. Why isn't more being done?"

186 American Cancer Society, "Hair Dyes and Cancer," November, 2022, https://www.cancer.org/healthy/cancer-causes/chemicals/hair-dyes.html

187 Tayo Bero, "Black women's hair products are killing us. Why isn't more being done?"

188 HC Editors, "Black Hair Types: Type 3 and Type 4 – What's Yours?" Hairstylecamp.com, September, 2022, https://hairstylecamp.com/black-hair-types/

189 The Toxic Twelve Chemicals and Contaminants in Cosmetics. https://www.ewg.org/the-toxic-twelve-chemicals-and-contaminants-in-cosmetics

190 https://www.ewg.org/skindeep/

191 S. Grogan, S. Gill, K. Brownbridge and A. Whalley, "Dress fit and body image: a thematic analysis of women's accounts during and after trying on dresses," *Body Image, 10* (2013): 380–388.

192 www.thecrownact.com

193 Lee, K. (2022). 6 Ways to Help Young Children Avoid Body Image Issues.

194 Melissa Lobo, "Staring Early: Instilling a Positive Body Image for Your Children," *Psychreg.org*, 2017.

195 Dawn Turner, "The message of Michelle Obama's new book is familiar but much needed," review of *The Light We Carry*, by Michelle Obama, The Washington Post, November 15, 2022.

Available at: https://www.washingtonpost.com/books/2022/11/15/michelle-obama-book/

About the Author:

MELINDA GORE is dedicated to quality of life improvement for women of color through health and wellness equity. As the founder of Her Wealth is Health, the premier online destination that prioritizes the health and well-being of Black women, she supports her clients in creating surroundings to promote healthy living and body positivity. Melinda is an author, speaker, certified health coach and diversity, inclusion and health equity practitioner.

Melinda has spent more than 20 years educating others to improve their quality of life with healthy habits and choices. Learn more about Melinda and her programs at www.melindagore.com.

"Body Image Boosters" Worksheets!

Grab your FREE copies today!

11 printable "Body Image Boosters" journal prompts
and exercises from
The Black Woman's Body Image Diet
help you put what you are learning into action, achieve more goals
and create body positive living.

Grab your FREE copy at www.freegiftfrommelinda.com

MOTIVATE AND INSPIRE OTHERS!

"Share This Book"

For special bulk pricing and to place an order
Contact: hello@melindagore.com

THE IDEAL PROFESSIONAL SPEAKER FOR YOUR NEXT EVENT

Any organization that wants to inspire their people to become "empowered" advocates of their personal health and well-being needs to hire Melinda Gore for a keynote and/or workshop training!

TO CONTACT OR BOOK MELINDA GORE TO SPEAK:
hello@melindagore.com

Printed in the USA
CPSIA information can be obtained
at www.ICGtesting.com
LVHW022138041023
760082LV00009B/322/J